OUTNUMBERED
OUTGUNNED
UNDETERRED

ROB JOHNSON

OUTNUMBERED
OUTGUNNED
UNDETERRED

TWENTY BATTLES AGAINST ALL ODDS

41 ILLUSTRATIONS, INCLUDING 20 BATTLE PLANS AND MAPS

Thames & Hudson

In memory of Professor Richard Holmes,
an inspiration

Frontispiece: Boer forces in the field during the Anglo-Boer War, 1900.

Copyright © 2011 Thames & Hudson Ltd, London

First published in 2011 in hardcover in the United States of America by
Thames & Hudson Inc., 500 Fifth Avenue, New York, New York 10110

thamesandhudsonusa.com

Library of Congress Catalog Card Number 2011922479

ISBN 978-0-500-25187-4

Printed in China by Toppan Leefung

CONTENTS

PREFACE

Why do some men and women, despite all the odds against them, decide to continue to resist, to endure and to take punishment? How is it that while some break and run, others provide inspirational courage, rally the discouraged and ultimately triumph? What are the attributes that enable some to endure and succeed where others fail? The resilience of the human spirit, the anatomy of courage and the setting of the highest example through leadership and personal sacrifice are among the most admirable virtues of the human race. Nowhere are these characteristics more thoroughly tested than in the crucible of war.

The purpose of this book is to illustrate, using twenty vivid case studies, some of the most epic actions of modern military history – situations where the odds were stacked against apparently weaker forces that found themselves either outnumbered, outgunned, in an impossible tactical situation or simply cut off from supplies. Yet, through determination, leadership, cunning, skill or sheer guts, many of these forces managed to achieve victory or earn the respect of their enemies. Some survived, others went down fighting.

In this book there are examples of sieges endured, stubborn defences mounted, attacks launched despite minimal strength, epic retreats and heroic last stands. Each story is told, analysed and accompanied by an illustration and map or battle plan that shows the main dispositions and the scale of the task facing the underdog. These examples cannot but inspire us, although the purpose of this book is not to create any romantic illusions of the business of war, simply collect together famous last stands or reiterate the well-known accounts of the Western canon. Rather it is to offer a critical history that has a resonance beyond the period in question, presenting a balance of interpretations and actions from across the globe that show less well-known actions have much to tell us about how the ability to succeed has affected the history of war.

We must not, however, forget that all these battles were fought by ordinary men, and sometimes women, who performed extraordinary feats under very specific and distinct circumstances. Their direct experiences may not be replicated. The lessons they hold for us lie in their evident ability to transmit their character and spirit under the greatest pressures. If, in the extreme crisis of war, human beings are capable of such resilience and prowess, we may reflect on how much we ourselves might achieve – or encourage others to achieve – when faced by danger and disaster.

Rob Johnson

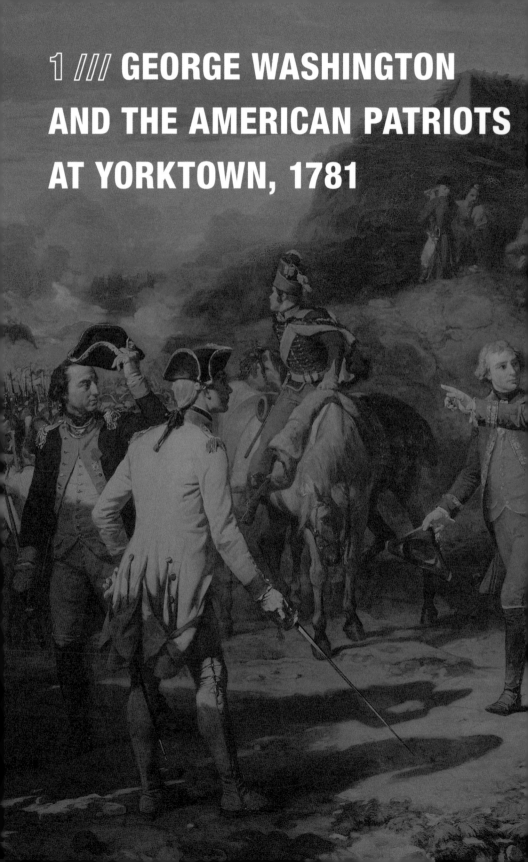

1 /// GEORGE WASHINGTON AND THE AMERICAN PATRIOTS AT YORKTOWN, 1781

*T*he decision to establish Valley Forge as a permanent base for the revolutionary American army, two years after the outbreak of war, kept alive the spirit of resistance despite the British regular forces ranged against them. Moreover, it provided a depot where Patriots could train and learn the art of war. For months their experiment in creating a standing army seemed close to collapse, but, in the end, a new American army emerged that would march to victory at Yorktown.

In the winter of 1777, the American colonists who had taken on the might of the British empire were in trouble. With supplies dwindling to a critical level their commander, George Washington, pleaded with Congress to provide food, clothing and shoes for his fledgling army as a matter of urgency. He wrote: 'unless some great and capital change suddenly takes place … this Army must inevitably … starve, dissolve or disperse, in order to obtain subsistence in the best manner they can'. Washington had taken his men into winter quarters so as to prevent the total collapse of his force. In previous winters, men had drifted away from their units in such numbers that it was almost impossible to maintain an army at all: this meant that they lacked cohesion when confronted by the British. Time and again they were driven from the field because they lacked the ability to function together effectively.

Washington's choice of Valley Forge in Pennsylvania as the location to keep his army intact over the winter was based on sound strategy. Having fought the Battle of White Marsh in December 1777, Washington's base protected the nearby farmlands of Pennsylvania from British raiding parties, but kept enough distance between him and the British army at Philadelphia to prevent a surprise attack. High ground, namely Mount Joy and Mount Misery, protected the site from the west, and the Schuylkill River provided both a defensive barrier to the north and a supply of fresh water. Hundreds of wooden huts had to be built to accommodate the 12,000 or so men at Valley Forge, while revetted earthworks strengthened the perimeter. The chief problem, though, was a lack of provisions. Food was scarce and, although fresh bread was sometimes available, soldiers were forced to depend on a mash of flour and water called 'firecake'. Supply of animal fodder was also intermittent, and many of the cavalry mounts and draught horses

Previous pages: **Painting of the Siege of Yorktown, 17 October 1781, by Louis-Charles-Auguste Couder.**

died in the cold weather. Uniforms were not available, and some of the troops were dressed in rags. In damp, fetid huts, inadequately fed and without winter clothing to keep out the cold, many men were incapacitated by disease. Typhoid, dysentery and pneumonia killed perhaps as many as 2,000, with a further 4,000 reported as unfit for duty. Inevitably, under such circumstances, many men began to desert.

In December 1777, Johann De Kalb wrote: 'Our men are infected with the Itch, a matter which attracts very little attention either in the hospitals or in the camp. I have seen poor fellows covered over and over with scab …. We … are already suffering from want of everything. The men have [had] neither meat nor bread for four days, and our horses are often left without any fodder.' A surgeon of the camp listed the problems in his private journal: 'Poor food – hard lodgings – cold weather – fatigue – nasty clothes – nasty cooking – smoked out of my sense – the devil's in it – I can't endure it – why are we sent here to starve and freeze? … here, all confusion – smoke and cold – hunger and filthiness …' He noted with bitterness that 'yesterday upwards of fifty officers resigned their commission'. The officers who left took their servants with them. Some commissary officers sold the camp's flour to the citizens of Philadelphia – or perhaps to the British. Soldiers simply abandoned their posts and used guard duty as an opportunity to run away from military service. Drunkenness and insubordination were serious problems.

Camp indiscipline extended to bad hygiene and the mishandling of supplies. In the orders of 13 March 1778, there was a note that 'the carcasses of dead horses are lying in and near the camp, and that the offals near many of the commissaries' stalls still lie unburied, that much filth and nastiness is spread amongst the huts, which are, or soon will be reduced to a state of putrefaction'. Criticism began to extend to Washington himself. While some blamed Congress, others, like the veteran fighter Major General Charles Lee, felt Washington was 'not fit to command a Sergeant's Guard'. But quarrels between the leading officers were not uncommon and several duels took place that winter.

Nevertheless, Washington did manage to retain a sizable portion of his force and to improve it throughout the first six months of 1778, and it is this achieve-ment that makes Valley Forge so significant. By doing so, Washington kept the flame of the Revolution alive. Indeed, his efforts made it possible to establish a more solid foundation for the American cause. Two elements in particular were crucial to his success: the involvement of patriotic citizens, especially the women; and the training programme implemented by Baron Friedrich Wilhelm von Steuben.

The camp followers of any eighteenth-century army were vitally important. In the absence of formal military services and logistics, women often acted as the victuallers, nurses, seamstresses and labourers of the force. These regimental camp followers were crucial to sustaining Washington's army at Valley Forge, not only providing rations and carrying out necessary repairs, but also bolstering the faltering morale of the troops. Billeted with the men, this little army of women and children prevented wholesale desertion.

The greatest contribution to the development of the army came from Baron von Steuben, a former Prussian army officer who had served under Frederick the Great. Washington quickly appointed the volunteer von Steuben to the duties of Acting Inspector General. Although the baron spoke almost no English, he realized that each American unit was using its own variation in drill, musketry and manoeuvre. Soon after his arrival in February 1778, von Steuben drew up his own drill and training manual, cutting the corners of the formal and long-winded European methods so as to standardize all practices. His staff translated the manual from von Steuben's French version and began to disseminate it. Von Steuben himself worked with individual units, often demonstrating drills and, through translators, taking time to explain the processes. The approach was considered revolutionary by some American officers, since soldiers had never been expected to understand drill and manoeuvre, only to obey. Though progressive, von Steuben was no saint: his poor command of English led to misunderstandings and frustrations, and he often exploded with rage. This so amused the troops that, in time, von Steuben learnt almost to caricature himself, using a mixture of threat and humour to win over the men.

The training was relentless. Parades started at six o'clock in the morning and continued for two hours. At nine, the parades began again for three hours. At noon, non-commissioned officers were trained, and instruction for the men ran all afternoon. Specialist tuition in tactics and leadership was given to the officers with a particular emphasis on their getting to know their men by name and character. There were lectures on camp hygiene, kitchen maintenance, changing bedding, washing. There were sessions set aside for the manufacture of weapons and gunpowder, for the repair of tools and arms, and for the construction of earthworks led by French engineers and Brigadier General Louis Duportail.

With sub-units mastering the discrete skills of marching in line and column, loading and firing and responding to commands, von Steuben turned to the movements and direction of larger formations. Companies, regiments and then brigades eventually learnt the business of battlefield drills. Von Steuben also recognized that the Patriots had hitherto feared the British bayonet charge, even when they occupied entrenched positions; he therefore introduced measures to build confidence and instil aggression into the American forces when making their own attacks with the bayonet. Von Steuben was thus responsible for the creation of a regular American army that could fight the British on their own terms and retain the field. Although the Patriots would continue to rely on irregular tactics and elements of guerrilla warfare, there was an understanding that victory could be achieved only by adopting the offensive and taking the fight to the British.

When France allied with the American revolutionaries in May 1778, this new regular force was augmented by European professionals both on land and at sea, greatly adding to their strength. The French alliance also had the effect of changing the British strategy completely: London could not afford to view the American colonies as the main theatre of operations when France posed a threat much closer to home. Moreover, Britain was more concerned with the protection of the West Indies and its colonial possessions in India from France, and so was forced to divert naval and land resources to these other regions.

The return of better weather and the emergence of a well-trained core at the new army at Valley Forge drew back men who had deserted over the winter. New volunteers also appeared, who were provided with fresh uniforms and integrated into the improved formations. A spirit and pride had evolved which could not easily be extinguished, and by the summer of 1778 the American army was able to take to the field with confidence.

In light of the French alliance the British, led by their recently commissioned commander Sir Henry Clinton, decided to quit Philadelphia and to fall back to New York. Unable to load his men aboard ships in the Delaware River because of a lack of transports, Clinton had to march the army overland. The column of troops and supply wagons extended over 12 miles (19 km), which made it vulnerable, and Washington felt the time had come to test his new Continental

Army. In stifling heat, the Americans tried to concentrate their forces and catch Clinton at Monmouth County Courthouse in the village of Freehold, New Jersey. The two sides clashed on 28 June 1778, but owing to Lee's hesitation the Americans were bundled back by British Grenadiers. Clinton and the British escaped intact, but the American army had been tempered in battle and it was only a matter of time before they made use of their training and experience to better effect.

In 1781, the British were still able to defeat the American forces sent against them. Quartermaster General Nathanael Greene (who had kept up a campaign of exhausting his British pursuers) was beaten at Guildford, Connecticut, on 15 March that year. But the tide was turning. Greene exemplified this transformation of the American resistance. In 1774 he had helped organize a local militia in Rhode Island, and used the opportunity to study military tactics at first hand. His natural talent for organizing was recognized by Washington, who had appointed him the commander of Boston in 1776, and Greene was also made responsible for constructing field fortifications at Long Island. He tried unsuccessfully to defend Fort Washington on the Hudson River, and took part in the battles of Trenton

Having allied with the French and built up their forces over several campaigns, the American Continental Army was finally able to bring greater numbers against the British. The capture of the two bastions near the walls on the right flank at Yorktown made the defences there untenable.

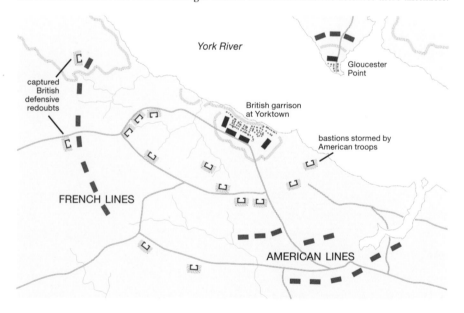

(New Jersey) and Germanstown (Pennsylvania) with varying success before becoming the Quartermaster General at Valley Forge. He continued his responsibilities for logistics and supply while commanding operations, but he resigned in protest at what he regarded as political interference in the supply of the army. However, the defeat of each of the armies in the south led to his urgent appointment as overall commander of the entire region from Delaware to Georgia, and Washington's second in command. In the space of just six years, he had risen from the rank of private in the Militia to Major General in the Continental Army.

When Greene took command of the south, his forces were in disarray. Dividing his troops to evade annihilation, he organized an escape march and managed to put his force across the Dan River out of reach of the British in February 1781. The following month, he tried to concentrate his various units again at Guildford Courthouse and, although driven from the field, inflicted such losses on the British that they were forced to fall back. He suffered further setbacks in battle, but nevertheless secured South Carolina. A self-trained soldier, Greene once remarked: 'We fight, get beat, rise, and fight again.'

The British were not able to afford this steady stream of casualties, and the Americans were able to muster more men to sustain their resistance. Furthermore, with French assistance, they had superior supplies of arms and munitions. In the late summer of 1781, the British General Cornwallis found his army outnumbered by a Franco-American force at Yorktown, Virginia. The arrival of a French fleet, which bested a covering British flotilla, prevented the relief of Cornwallis's garrison, and this encouraged the Americans to go on the offensive. Although Yorktown consisted of a series of entrenched bastions, connected with ramparts and ditches, the Americans enjoyed a superiority of firepower and on the first day alone, they fired 3,600 round shot into the defences. Cornwallis concluded that, with his ragged force 'against so powerful an attack ... [we could] not hope to make a very long resistance'. He had only 3,250 men fit for duty, and the rest of the garrison was forced to shelter below the sandy river cliffs to avoid destruction. The Continental Army daily inched its guns closer to the main defences, eventually reducing the range to 300 yards (275 m). No man could stand on the parapets without being shot down.

On 14 October, one French and one American battalion made a night attack on two vital bastions on the left of the British line. Night operations are complex and usually guarantee success only if the personnel are well trained. It is a testament to the progress made since Valley Forge that the Americans executed such a textbook attack so efficiently. One soldier recalled how he and his comrades had 'arrived at the trenches a little before sunset' and that before dark every man was 'informed of the whole plan'. The first line consisted of sappers armed with axes, whose job was to cut through the abattis (a fortification made with sharpened wooden sticks); this cleared the way for the assault troops behind, led by officers with bayonets fixed to long staves. The soldier continued: 'at dark the detachment … advanced beyond the trenches and lay down on the ground to await the signal for the attack, which was to be three shells from a certain battery … all three batteries in our line were silent, and we lay anxiously waiting for the signal.'

Their cool discipline was tested to the extreme when at last the signal guns opened fire, 'three shells with their fiery trains mounting the air in quick succession – the word "up", "up", was then reiterated through the detachment. We moved towards the redoubt we were to attack with unloaded muskets.' As the Americans and French dashed forward the British sentries made a vain attempt to stem the rush, but within moments the Americans were scrambling over the banks into the first bastion. The fight was quickly settled, and the two redoubts carried. Cornwallis wrote to Clinton that 'our situation now becomes very critical; we dare not show a gun to their old batteries and I expect that their new ones will open tomorrow morning'. In fact, the British garrison was already down to the last of its meagre rations. The defences were strewn with the dismembered dead. Farriers made daily rounds to execute dying horses. Some soldiers deserted. Cornwallis made one last desperate attempt to save his small force. As 350 men made a heroic but hopeless sortie against the nearest batteries, the advanced party of the garrison slipped across the York River to Gloucester Point. As the second wave prepared themselves a storm blew up and scattered the small boats. With all hopes of escape lost, and with the Americans renewing their terrific cannonade against the crumbling earthen ramparts, Cornwallis sought to tender terms of surrender. The British troops, some weeping, others angrily casting down their arms, were nevertheless surprised to find themselves treated with 'astonishing kindness' by both American and French soldiers.

The British capitulation at Yorktown did not conclude the American Revolutionary War, but the event did mark the completion of a process of professionalization of the American army. It was also a clear victory for the Patriots after years of setbacks and defeats. At Valley Forge, the Revolution had seemed in danger of collapse, but the achievement of that encampment was to sustain and then develop a new army, whose success at Yorktown indicated that the Americans had gained the upper hand in the struggle. From this point onwards, backed by the French army and navy, the revolutionaries could withstand the British. Just two years later, in 1783, the war was concluded, and the Americans had realized their dream of independence. The transformation of the army at Valley Forge established an important symbolic principle during the Revolution – namely, that, despite the odds against them, American citizens had it within their power to determine the course of their own history. Valley Forge became more than a mere training depot: it was the springboard for a sense of national achievement.

2 /// THE UNITED STATES MARINES AT TRIPOLI, 1803–5

During the American Revolutionary War (1775–83), the shipping of the American colonies was still under the protection of the British Royal Navy and, after the alliance with France in 1778, French ships also acted as guarantors of American cargoes. At that time the greatest threat to American and European shipping came from the corsairs of the Barbary Coast, where pirates enjoyed the support of Muslim North Africa, namely the sultanates of Morocco and Algiers, and the principalities of Tunis and Tripoli. Ruthless piratical crews kept up an unrelenting offensive at sea against all merchant traffic, taking booty and slaves as they chose. The Muslim rulers who launched these proxy raiders enjoyed a lucrative share of the profits and justified their criminal activity as part of a more laudable struggle against all infidels. The rogue states' wealth, and their remoteness from the centre of the Ottoman empire, to which they owed a nominal suzerainty, meant that they were a law unto themselves.

For decades the Europeans had attempted to contain the problem and the Knights of Malta had been specially commissioned by the Catholic Church to defend the continent against the Turks. Younger knights had, nevertheless, chosen to wage war against the Barbary pirates. In doing so the knights amassed considerable booty and wealth, a fact which caught the attention of the ambitious Napoleon Bonaparte in the 1790s. Napoleon's actions in the Mediterranean were to have severe repercussions for the nascent United States. He planned to take control of Egypt as a staging post against the British in India and Southeast Asia, and designed his own imperial dominion to replace them. In 1798, Napoleon seized Malta and stripped the island of its wealth. At a stroke, Europe's southern coastline was once again vulnerable to waves of Barbary corsairs.

At first there seemed no immediate threat to American interests because the United States had shared a close, if informal, amity with Morocco since the latter opened its ports to US ships in 1777. The United States also paid yearly tributes to the Barbary nations, and ratified these informal relations by signing treaties with Morocco (1786), Tripoli (1796) and Algeria (1797). These payments and agreements did not, however, stop the corsairs taking men and ships hostage and demanding ransoms, payments that added a further financial burden. Thomas Jefferson, America's ambassador to France, wanted to revoke the treaty and advocated

Previous pages: Burning of the frigate *Philadelphia* in the harbour of Tripoli, 16 February 1804. Colour lithograph.

building up a navy to patrol the sea lanes instead. However, many in Congress, believing that Americans should focus on the development of their huge hinterland, marginalized the Atlantic and Mediterranean trade routes, and opposed the creation of a large navy.

The Barbary (a corruption of the term 'berber') corsairs, had been raiding southern and western Europe for 200 years, seizing ships' cargoes and enslaving Christians. Those who resisted were treated with considerable cruelty and summarily executed. Such was the scourge that sections of the Mediterranean coastline were depopulated, and it is estimated that 800,000 Europeans were taken into captivity. By the late eighteenth century, however, more powerful navies began to check the activities of the Barbary raiders. English and Dutch fleets had inflicted significant defeats on the Barbary corsairs and Tripoli and Algiers were subjected to bombardments. Despite this, slave-raiding and attacks on merchant ships continued.

In 1801, Yusuf Pasha Karamanli of Tripoli demanded a substantial increase in tribute from America, but the election of Jefferson as president marked a change in foreign policy and he refused to pay. Tripoli promptly declared war and Jefferson sent several frigates into the Mediterranean. In August, the USS *Enterprise* intercepted the corsair vessel *Tripoli* and captured her. Despite this, it was not until 1803, when Commodore Edward Preble maintained a blockade of the Barbary ports and made sorties against their harbours and ships, that hostilities began in earnest. The war did not begin auspiciously for the Americans. The naval blockade, though attracting the support of Sweden, proved ineffective. A series of setbacks then damaged the Americans' position. The personal secretary of the British Governor of Malta was killed in a duel by an American captain, which so soured relations with the United Kingdom that Preble was deprived of an important nearby base for resupply. In early 1803, an accidental explosion aboard an American ship killed 19 men. In May that year, a large squadron of American warships was assembled and set out for Tripoli to destroy the Corsairs' fleet at anchor. Large shore guns protected the Barbary fleet, which meant that Marines had to be landed close to the walls of the city. They managed to set fire to many of the ships, but large crowds of civilians assembled and showered the Americans with stones and harassing fire. One group of Tripolitans ran the gauntlet of the withdrawing Americans and their covering squadron to extinguish the fires on their ships.

Early in 1804, the Americans' luck began to change. The Kingdom of the Two Sicilies declared war on Tripoli, which gave them the support of small, manoeuvrable gunboats. On 3 August, an American-led combined force made another attack, bombarding Tripoli at close range. The Americans aboard the smaller gunboats used their speed to catch up with the swift Barbary vessels, boarding them and engaging the pirates in hand-to-hand combat. After destroying part of the port's fortifications, a large mosque and several gunboats, the squadron withdrew.

The following year, in one of these operations, the USS *Philadelphia* ran aground in Tripoli harbour and was soon under intense gunfire from shore batteries. Tripolitan ships joined the bombardment and, despite their desperate efforts, the crew were unable to refloat the warship. Captain William Bainbridge took the difficult decision to capitulate in order the save the lives of his men, a considerable risk since so many captives of the Barbary pirates had been forced into slavery. The men were taken ashore to learn their fate. There was a chance that the ship could be refitted and used as a powerful weapon against the Americans, but in fact the *Philadelphia*, stuck fast, was converted into a platform for a Tripolitan gun battery.

It was under these circumstances that a daring plan was conceived among the American fleet. Stung by the surrender of the *Philadelphia* to their enemies, Lieutenant Stephen Decatur led out a small detachment of Marines to recover the ship or, at least, to put her out of action. The odds of success were very small, and indeed the chances of Decatur and his men surviving the raid seemed slim. The Tripolitans were alert to the threat of American vessels sailing into the harbour, and had guns that ringed the port. They possessed a sizable garrison that could reinforce any part of the city. Nevertheless, the men set out during the night of 16 February 1804, using the captured ketch *Mastico* – appropriately renamed the USS *Intrepid* – to disguise their approach.

The deception plan succeeded and they sailed into the harbour. Decatur's small party was able to board the *Philadelphia* and overcame all resistance. It was then a race against time to disable the vessel permanently, before the Tripolitans could react. They set fires, which took hold of the beached ship, and made good their escape, protected by American ships coming in at dawn.

With the *Philadelphia* destroyed, the Americans made a series of naval assaults on the port in 1804, but none of them neutralized the Tripolitan shipping entirely. Master Commandant Richard Somers volunteered to command the *Intrepid* as a fire

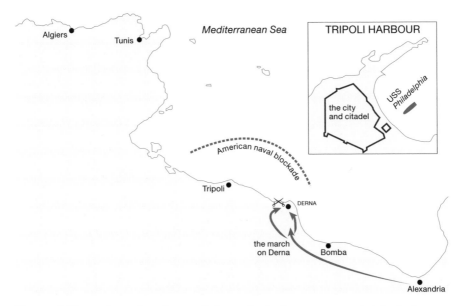

Eaton and O'Bannon's march on Derna split into a classic pincer manoeuvre to take the town. At the top right can be seen a plan of Tripoli port, showing the location of the grounded USS *Philadelphia* and the scene of Decatur's daring raid.

ship and planned to sail it, filled with gunpowder, into the packed enemy ships in a raid even more hazardous than Decatur's. Tragically, Somers and his crew were all killed before their mission could be completed. Tripolitan guns hammered the *Intrepid*, and the powder detonated before it could reach the ships in the harbour.

Unable to defeat the Tripolitans decisively from the sea, the American strategy was to initiate a change of regime instead. William Eaton, the former Consul to Tunis, was charged with replacing the ruler of Tripoli, Yusuf Karamanli, with his elder brother and the rightful heir, Hamet. Eaton recruited a force of 500 Arab, Greek and Berber mercenaries at Alexandria and appointed Lieutenant Presley O'Bannon as their American commander. On 8 March the contingent set out to make an arduous 500-mile (800-km) march across the North African desert, knowing that they would have to fight their way through Barbary forces at the end of the odyssey. The 50-day ordeal tested the patience of the mercenaries and several times they threatened mutiny. Nevertheless, in the April of 1805, Eaton and O'Bannon's force reached the port city of Bomba, 38 miles (60 km) southeast of the Tripolitan port of Derna – their target. At Bomba they made a rendezvous with three American warships. Rested and resupplied, the American-led contingent had the satisfaction of watching these ships shell the defences of Derna, but all knew that this strategically important location would need to be stormed from the landward side.

On 27 April a two-pronged assault was launched. The Arab detachment led by Hamet circled around to the west and began their attack in the direction of the governor's palace, while O'Bannon, a handful of American Marines and the rest of the mercenaries began a direct assault on the harbour fortress. Alerted to the impending attack, the more numerous defenders had strengthened their position and they managed to repel the first American wave. Eaton himself joined the attack and the ferocity of the second attempt caused the defenders to flee. O'Bannon mounted the ramparts and raised the Stars and Stripes to signal their success to the warships, while his men turned the captured cannon on their former owners. The defenders retreated through the city and were intercepted by Hamet's Arab mercenaries. The port was taken in just under two hours. The newly instated Prince Harmet Karamanli was so impressed with O'Bannon's achievements that it is said he presented him with a magnificent curved sword. Later, when he returned to the United States, the Virginia Legislature presented O'Bannon with a similar sword of honour in the curved Mameluke style, and in 1825 the Marine Corps adopted the design as the dress sword for all officers.

Although the battle had been won, the campaign was far from over. Yusuf dispatched reinforcements to Derna, and the port was quickly encircled. Eaton ordered that the fortifications be strengthened but his small contingent could not be strong everywhere. On 13 May the Tripolitans tried to storm the town, driving the Arab mercenaries back almost to the governor's palace. Eaton directed the town's guns and naval fire onto the Tripolitans as they advanced and this broke up their attack. There were several further attempts like this to retake the port, but each one was driven off. By the beginning of June, Eaton felt sufficiently confident to renew the offensive. He led a second desert march, hoping to close on Tripoli itself, but the signing of a peace treaty prevented this final, daring plan from being executed. The terms of the treaty were controversial, but Tripoli was forced to relinquish 300 American prisoners, for which they were paid $60,000. Tripoli remained cowed for two years, until a new round of piracy led to a Second Barbary War in 1815.

The epic struggle with the Barbary pirates was the first occasion on which the newly independent United States conducted operations on foreign soil in defence of its national interests. It was a war marked by acts of astonishing courage in the face of considerable odds. Lieutenant Decatur's gallant raid on the *Philadelphia* was praised by Britain's Horatio Nelson, the victor of the battles of the Nile and Trafalgar, as 'the most bold and daring act of the age'. Somers's equally courageous act was denied success but illustrated the remarkable spirit of the new American navy. Eaton and O'Bannon demonstrated incredible endurance and determination in their desert march to Derna, and, against the odds, they succeeded in seizing and holding a strategic port against far greater numbers of enemy forces. Rightly, the United States Navy and Marine Corps are proud of these pioneering achievements, which set such a high standard.

3 /// NAPOLEON'S SIX DAYS' CAMPAIGN, FRANCE, 1814

Although his forces were outnumbered by the Coalition armies closing in on him, Napoleon's campaign of 1814 was one of the finest demonstrations of his strategic and tactical skill. There were several significant battles, almost all of which Napoleon won against the odds, but perhaps the most prominent feature of the fighting was his ability to inspire his men to continue to resist despite crippling losses, punishing marches and diminishing supplies.

Driven out of Russia in 1812, and forced to relinquish control of central Europe the following year, Napoleon Bonaparte, Emperor of the French, faced the prospect of defeat as his Sixth Coalition enemies (formed by Austria, Prussia, Sweden, Britain and certain German states) massed on the borders. To defend the 300-mile (480-km) frontier of France that ran along the Rhine, Napoleon could muster no more than 80,000 ragged and exhausted men. Inside the German states were 100,000 French troops, but they were scattered or besieged, unable to reach France ahead of their enemies. Directly across the Rhine, facing Napoleon, were 300,000 Coalition invasion troops, consisting of the armies of Russia, Austria and Prussia. On the southern borders, General Sir Arthur Wellesley (soon to become the Duke of Wellington) was driving the French back across the Franco-Spanish frontier, while Napoleon's troops in Italy were outmanoeuvred and unable to fall back to protect the homeland. Former French allies among the German states and the Netherlands were also beginning to desert Napoleon.

Napoleon set about raising more men to meet the invasion, with the energy that had made him so famous in the 1790s. He called up 900,000 conscripts, the French National Guard, the *gendarmerie* and even forestry officials. He demanded that his staff find the necessary arms and equipment for this hastily formed force, and considered issuing pikes where there were not enough muskets. He increased the size of his elite Imperial Guard, stripping the most experienced men from old regiments to give himself a reliable core among the legions of new and untried recruits. Napoleon, the great advocate of mass in battle, now faced armies far larger than his own and he was desperate to balance the odds. There was a chorus of propaganda, exhorting greater efforts for the defence of *la Patrie* ('the fatherland'); he recalled the drafts of troops that were en route to Italy and Spain, and conscripted young men who were not due to serve for another two years.

Previous pages: **Napoleon's campaign to defend France in 1814. Painting by Jean-Louis Ernest Meissonier.**

However, Napoleon did not meet his targets. Of the 900,000 called up, only 120,000 mustered for service. A war-weary population refused to pay taxes. There were not enough guns or horses for the cavalry and the artillery. Worse, Joachim Murat, Marshal of France, who was at that time stationed in the Kingdom of Naples, went over to the allies. This defection ended any chance Napoleon might have had to repeat his strategic success of 1797, when he had boldly swung through northern Italy to defeat the Austrians and break the allied Coalition. Even Napoleon's diplomacy failed: he had offered to restore King Ferdinand VII of Spain to his throne, hoping this move would split the allies in acrimonious debate, but the plan failed. Despite his numerous disadvantages, Napoleon continued to make strategic calculations that relied on his military prowess as a commander. When he was told he must restore the Netherlands to their independence and guarantee the peace – which represented an opportunity to rescue the situation – he rejected the demand. Even though fortune was against him, Napoleon preferred to fight his enemies to a standstill and impose his own terms from a position of strength. Thus, the Coalition invasion began in January 1814, with three converging thrusts aimed at Paris, and the French set about preparing to meet the overwhelming onslaught.

Napoleon planned to defeat each enemy army in detail. Karl Philipp, the Prince of Schwarzenberg and Austrian commander, had 210,000 men crossing the Upper Rhine, while Jean-Baptiste Bernadotte (a former French marshal, who had turned against Napoleon to become king of Sweden) brought 60,000 soldiers through the Netherlands. The Prussians, led by Marshal Gebhard Blücher, marched with 75,000 men through Lorraine. In response, Napoleon sent a corps of 30,000 inexperienced troops against one wing of Blücher's army on 29 January 1814. The Prussians were obliged to withdraw when threatened from a flank, but Blücher counter-attacked at La Rothière on 1 February, massing 116,000 Coalition troops against Napoleon's 40,000. Napoleon tried to extricate the army but was forced to fight in the drifting snow until darkness allowed his men to slip away. A blizzard made it difficult to maintain direction, and some units resorted to hand-to-hand fighting with bayonets when the wet conditions left their gunpowder damp. The short but aggressive fight had cost the two sides 6,000 casualties and, by all calculations, Napoleon seemed to be beaten. The allies resumed their march on Paris with some confidence.

Then, contrary to all expectations, Napoleon launched a lightning series of battles known as the Six Days' Campaign in a deteriorating strategic situation and against much greater numbers. Starting on 10 February, he struck against the Prussians, who were strung out in an extended line of march. He attacked General Zakhar Olsufiev at Champaubert, east of Paris, inflicting 4,000 casualties on a force that had taken the field with 5,000 men.

On 11 February, Napoleon immediately marched on two more elements of the allied army at Montmirail, namely the corps of General Ludwig Yorck and General Dmitri Sacken. Initially Napoleon had only 10,500 men available (consisting of the Imperial Guard with a few conscripts) against the 18,000 in Sacken's command. But stationing some men to watch for the arrival of Yorck, Napoleon called for all available reinforcements until he had mustered a total of 20,000 men, then he launched an all-out attack. Sacken was driven back, but as the battle progressed, the Coalition forces under Yorck arrived and Napoleon's plan appeared to be in jeopardy. Then, Napoleon's corps commander, Marshal Édouard Mortier, arrived with reinforcements just in time to check and then drive back Yorck's force.

The next day, Napoleon pursued Yorck's rearguard as far as Château-Thierry on the Marne River. There, Michel Ney, Napoleon's most courageous marshal, made a furious assault, pierced the allied lines and captured heights above and beyond them. The attack was so impetuous that two regiments of Russian cavalry were cut off and compelled to surrender, although the Prussian infantry got away thanks to the covering fire of their artillery. Remarkably, in three days of fighting, Napoleon had suffered only 3,450 killed in action, while the allies had incurred losses of over 10,000. To ensure a decisive victory over the Prussians, Napoleon made one final thrust against Blücher, intending thereafter to march against Schwarzenberg.

Napoleon had set out to locate Blücher at 0300 hours on 14 February with the Imperial Guard and the cavalry in his vanguard. The leading Prussian corps, under Lieutenant General Friedrich von Kleist, numbered 20,000 men and had clashed with French outposts at Vauchamps as it sought out Napoleon's main body of men. The Prussian cavalry was driven off, but they secured a prisoner who informed von Kleist and Blücher that Napoleon's main force was indeed in the area. While the allies were deliberating, Napoleon was already quickly gathering his formations to concentrate 25,000 men for yet another decisive battle. When it became apparent to Blücher that the Prussians did not have local superiority in numbers, he began to withdraw. Marshal Emmanuel de Grouchy, leading the bulk of Napoleon's cavalry, attempted to swing behind the Prussians and cut off their line of retreat, but the broken ground slowed the manoeuvre so that the Prussians were able to fight their way back and Blücher escaped. Nevertheless, the confused withdrawal cost the allies another 7,000 casualties and 16 guns, while French losses numbered only 6,000.

Despite these tactical victories, Paris was still threatened by a vast Austrian force, and Napoleon had to force-march for two days to catch up with the allies on the Seine. His exhausted men had covered 60 miles (95 km) in mid-winter conditions, and, on arrival, they were pitched straight into battle. On 17 February at Nangis, the Coalition corps of the Russian General Peter Wittgenstein was surprised and routed, throwing the Bavarians, who were in support of them, into disorder. The Austrians attempted to make a withdrawal, despite their greater numbers, leaving a covering force under the Prince of Württemberg at Montereau. Any hope of an organized withdrawal was thwarted, however, when the French opened up with a massed battery of guns, then launched columns of infantry at the town, which fell after a sharp fight. Another 2,500 Frenchmen lay dead or dying on the field, but Schwarzenberg had been persuaded to hold his main force 40 miles (65 km) back, and Napoleon had bought himself a little more time.

Nevertheless, Napoleon soon learnt that Blücher had recovered and the Prussians were on the move again, meaning the French would have to switch their axis a third time. Napoleon detached a portion of his force to delay Schwarzenberg, then hastened after Blücher who was within 25 miles (40 km) of the capital. But Schwarzenberg understood the relentless logic of time, numbers and position: as soon as Napoleon left to tackle the Prussians, he resumed his advance on Paris. Napoleon's covering force was defeated at Bar-sur-Aube on 27 February.

Blücher was advancing along the River Marne with 85,000 men when Napoleon caught up with him. The Prussian Field Marshal had anticipated an impetuous attack, and planned to pin Napoleon down long enough for the Russian General Ferdinand von Wintzingerode to outflank him with overwhelming numbers. But Napoleon moved too fast for him. Pinning Blücher at Craonne, the

French executed a dramatic flank assault on 7 March. The old Marshal was forced to withdraw, albeit in good order, inflicting some 5,000 casualties on Napoleon's dwindling forces. Blücher still hoped to outwit his adversary. At Laon, on 9 March, Blücher halted and deployed his entire force against Napoleon, who could only muster half their numbers with a force that consisted of thousands of raw conscripts. Boldly, Napoleon sent 9,500 men under Marshal Auguste de Marmont on a flanking move, while his main body made a frontal assault.

Marmont's inexperienced men struggled to get into position and were in turn outflanked by Yorck's corps, which had been carefully positioned in advance. Marmont was soon in trouble, trying to extricate his men under fire. It was only the defiant stand of a company of guardsmen at the Festieux Defile against Prussian cavalry, and a voluntary counter-attack by Colonel Etienne Fabvier's battalion (supported by just two cannon) that saved the situation. Napoleon continued to hammer away until evening, but he had no troops available for any further manoeuvres. Still his men followed him doggedly. He withdrew, leaving behind another 6,000 killed and wounded, and made his way to Soissons.

There, Napoleon learnt of the fall of Rheims and the continued allied advance on Paris. Although suffering a variety of ailments and worn out by weeks of furious preparation and campaigning, Napoleon hurled himself at the task of retaking the old city in an attempt to sever the allies' line of communication, and thereby halt their move towards Paris. On 13 March, Napoleon appeared before Rheims and routed the Russian corps under Emmanuel St Priest. The move, brilliantly concealed and speedily executed, had given him a position astride the line of communication of both Schwarzenberg and Blücher, just as he had hoped. Exhibiting the tough good humour of his old campaigns, he joked: 'I am still the man I was at Wagram and Austerlitz.'

Schwarzenberg, who had intercepted Napoleon's dispatches and therefore knew his plans, nevertheless decided to continue his advance on Paris. This forced the French to chase him. On 20 March, with his troop numbers dwindling from fatigue and combat, Napoleon struck at the Austrians near Arcis-sur-Aube. The Austrians spent the night reinforcing their advance guard so that, as dawn broke, 80,000 Coalition troops confronted Napoleon's remaining 28,000 men. Schwarzenberg initially hoped Napoleon would attack, but when Napoleon seemed inactive, he felt unsure of himself and allowed the French to filter back across the River Aube. Realizing that Napoleon was getting away, the Austrians belatedly launched an attack in the afternoon, but Napoleon and his tired little army escaped.

On 25 March, Napoleon's rearguard (under Marshals Mortier and Marmont) was defeated in the Battle of Fère-Champenoise. The French National Guard gallantly went down fighting in the action, losing 3,500 out of their original strength of 4,000. Napoleon's force was no longer sufficiently strong to defend the capital, or to defeat the allied armies in the field. Nevertheless, the Paris National Guard made a brave stand at Clichy until driven back to Montmartre. Marmont and his 500 remaining troops held on for as long as possible, but the allied numbers were overwhelming and he accepted defeat on the outskirts of Paris. Lieutenant Viaux of the 2nd Grenadiers of the Guards, an invalid, gathered twenty comrades at Montmartre for a defiant, but ultimately hopeless last stand in which they all lost their lives. Outside the capital, Napoleon and his guardsmen were still spoiling for a fight, but Ney and the other senior officers (along with the surviving members of the army) had had enough. Paris was occupied by 145,000 allied

With allied armies (grey) advancing from every direction, Napoleon's outnumbered forces fought a desperate rearguard action back to the gates of Paris. The French demonstrated great courage, tenacity and skilful manoeuvre throughout the campaign.

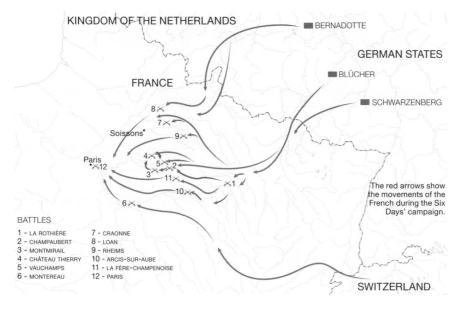

KINGDOM OF THE NETHERLANDS

■ BERNADOTTE

GERMAN STATES

FRANCE

■ BLÜCHER

■ SCHWARZENBERG

Soissons•

8 ✕
7 ✕
9 ✕

Paris
•✕12

4 ✕
5 ✕ ✕ 2
3 ✕
11 ✕
10 ✕
✕ 1
6 ✕

The red arrows show the movements of the French during the Six Days' campaign.

BATTLES

1 – LA ROTHIÈRE	7 – CRAONNE
2 – CHAMPAUBERT	8 – LOAN
3 – MONTMIRAIL	9 – RHEIMS
4 – CHÂTEAU THIERRY	10 – ARCIS-SUR-AUBE
5 – VAUCHAMPS	11 – LA FÈRE-CHAMPENOISE
6 – MONTEREAU	12 – PARIS

SWITZERLAND

troops and Napoleon, deciding to reject the offers from his loyalists to start a guerrilla war, abdicated.

Even then, Napoleon was not finished. With each of the European allies ranged against him, still discussing their plans for a post-Napoleonic 'restored' continent, Napoleon escaped from his island prison on Elba less than a year after being incarcerated there. On 1 March 1815, he landed in France with just 200 men: the most loyal of his grognards from the old Imperial Guard. Even though French civilians were cautious and sometimes hostile to Napoleon's return, there was little support for the royalists of the House of Bourbon either. The French army was perhaps the key to the whole venture, and Napoleon knew it. Confronted at Grenoble, Napoleon appealed to his soldiers' loyalty and was received with great enthusiasm. The little force grew to 14,000 as it advanced on Paris. Veterans set off from their towns and villages to rejoin the 'Eagles', while some of the senior officers (conscious that they had betrayed their Emperor in 1814 to join the new Bourbon regime) fled into exile. Within weeks Napoleon had raised an army of 124,000 fit to take the field, with 100,000 in depots and 300,000 in training. The allies were forced to respond, recreate their own armies, advance on the French frontiers and again march against Napoleon.

Napoleon inflicted a temporary defeat on Blücher at Ligny on 16 June 1815, before turning to confront the Anglo-Dutch-Belgian army at Waterloo two days later. Even this battle, Napoleon's final defeat, was, in the words of the victorious commander, the Duke of Wellington: 'the nearest run thing you ever saw in your life'. Napoleon had come very close to resurrecting his entire political apparatus and might, in time, have intimidated his rivals into some sort of accommodation both in domestic and foreign affairs. His resilience, his capacity for decisive action and his sheer determination against all the odds serve to make Napoleon an inspirational figure. In 1814, Napoleon had proved that he possessed the tactical skill and loyalty of his troops by confronting and defeating vast numbers of enemy forces. Through speed and manoeuvre he was able to outmarch and outwit his adversaries. Although Napoleon was unable to alter the deteriorating strategic situation, it is remarkable that he was able to command such a presence among his troops. Critics continue to dissect his errors and personal flaws, but his achievements, particularly in 1814, remain undiminished. Wellington, who believed that Napoleon should have kept his forces concentrated in 1814, nevertheless concluded that the Six Days' Campaign that year was all 'very brilliant, probably the ablest of all his performances'.

4 /// SIMÓN BOLÍVAR AND THE LIBERATION MOVEMENT, SOUTH AMERICA, 1813–25

*I*n the early nineteenth century, the chances of South Americans gaining their independence from their colonists, primarily Spain and Portugal, seemed very slim. The Great Powers (France, Austria, Russia and the United Kingdom) were not interested in waging war on their behalf, even when they opposed Spain in Europe, and furthermore the South American states were bitterly divided among themselves. There was no sense of national identity, and even the educated elites feared disorder within the masses more than they wished to see the overthrow of colonial authorities. When republican leaders such as Simón Bolívar emerged, they were compelled to shore up their legitimacy among their peers repeatedly. Bolívar himself was defeated time and again, yet refused to give up. With relatively small forces, battling both the royalist armies and the inhospitable environment, Bolívar linked up with other liberation leaders and eventually achieved his ambition of an independent South America. Bolívar himself was descended from the earliest colonists, his family having built up its wealth through farming large estates or managing gold and copper mines. The death of his parents when he was a child led to Bolívar's early entry into the military academy in Venezuela, where he studied tactics and armaments. He found himself on a visit to Paris on 2 December 1804 – the precise moment of the coronation of Napoleon Bonaparte. It seems that by the time of his return to South America, Bolívar was profoundly affected by the nationalist sentiments that had been prevalent in France.

The catalyst for the South American wars of independence was the French occupation of Spain in 1808. Charles IV of Spain abdicated, leaving the colonies with neither a head of state nor a centralized government. By 1810, juntas had formed across the continent, but many were merely looking for ways to maintain the old order. One exception was the Junta of Caracas, which announced the independence of Venezuela in 1811. The declaration sparked rebellions in favour of the Bourbon monarchy in Spain, but the arrival of royalist forces from the west led to the collapse of the Junta in 1812. The republicans were deported and colonial authority was restored. Bolívar, who had served as a colonel for the Junta, had been defeated at San Felipe Fort when royalist prisoners broke out and seized the magazine, and his small contingent had been overwhelmed.

Previous pages: Engraving showing the Battle of Boyacá.

Despite being exiled, Bolívar made his way to Cartagena de Indias, another state that had declared its independence. Here, four other provinces joined the cause to form the United Provinces of New Granada, and Bolívar enlisted in the new army that had been created. He was soon in action, leading troops against towns in Cartagena that resisted the Union, and successes here caught the attention of the new republican authorities. Bolívar used this repute to lobby for a campaign against the royalists in Venezuela, and in May 1813 he was granted permission to launch his 'Admirable Campaign'.

The challenge for Bolívar was that the Venezuelans were unlikely to greet his arrival as a 'liberation' at all. Many had abandoned their sympathies for the republicans, and the few brave enough to espouse the cause were tortured or killed by royalist forces. Wealthy individuals in particular had had their property looted and were beaten or murdered. Bolívar elected to fight fire with fire and issued his 'Decree of War to the Death', threatening to kill anyone who opposed him. In fact, the royalist troops were hardly a reliable force and Bolívar's army was able to defeat them in a series of sharp actions outside Caracas. The capital fell to the republicans on 6 August 1813 and there were reprisals against the royalist diehards. Before Bolívar could consolidate his grip on power, however, the southern rural population, the *llaneros*, were roused to rebellion. Captain General Juan Manuel Cajigal commanded royalist troops in the region, but it was José Tomás Boves who led the vast irregular llanero hordes. At the Battle of La Puerta (15 June 1814), the republicans were overwhelmed and Caracas fell the next day. Retreating to the east, Bolívar's army was cut to pieces at the Battle of Aragua de Barcelona (18 August 1814): most of the 3,000 men under his command were killed or wounded by a force over three times the size of his own. The survivors were soon encircled, and Bolívar was relieved of his command and sent into exile for a second time.

While many in his position would have given up, Bolívar refused to contemplate anything but victory. Even when the Spaniards sent an expeditionary force of 10,000 men to reinforce the royalist cause, and New Granada looked as if it might be overrun, Bolívar rejoined the army of the United Provinces and marched on Bogotá. This he captured on 12 December 1814 after an eight-month campaign, but, poised to strike north against the main royalist stronghold of Santa Marta, the New Granadans started to dispute the best way forward and the divided republicans were compelled to retreat. Within two years, Bogotá and Cartagena had fallen back into royalist hands and Bolívar was again forced into exile, this time to Jamaica. He appealed to Great Britain for assistance, but got none. The cause of independence seemed to be lost.

Support came from an unlikely quarter. The small and impoverished republic of Haiti offered money, arms and volunteers, while a warship was acquired from England for much-needed transport and firepower. Landing at Ocumare de la Costa on 6 July 1816, Bolívar announced the restoration of the Venezuelan republic and the emancipation of all slaves. At first, the expeditionary sortie was successful, taking a number of small ports, but soon Bolívar was routed and forced to retreat back to Haiti. Undaunted, he raised new troops and sailed from Jacmel in December 1816 to rejoin the republicans still clinging to the mainland.

At Angostura, the republicans had been too weak to conclude a siege, but the arrival of Bolívar's modest reinforcements proved just enough to tip the balance. This former royalist stronghold gave the patriots, as they were now styled, a firm base of operations. Bolívar then initiated his strategic communications campaign by publishing *Correo del Orinoco*, a newspaper that was circulated throughout Europe and South America. Mindful of the

Caribbean Sea

Santa Marta
Carta Negra
CARABOBO
Caracas
ARAGUA DE BARCELONA
LA PUERTA
Angostura
CÚCUTA
BOGOTÁ
BOYACÁ
VARGAS SWAMP
UNION OF NEW GRANADA (1822)
Quito
PICHINCHA
BRAZIL
PERU (1824)
JUNIN
LIMA
AYACUCHO
BOLIVIA (1825)
Pacific Ocean

The wars of liberation in South America were protracted. Both sides were hindered by the terrain and environment, and by populations who had not polarized in their sympathies: Bolivar had to make repeated attempts to drive Spain out.

previous disasters, Bolívar and his allies began to recruit the llaneros, their former enemies, as auxiliaries to their army; however, the multiple factions within the republican ranks forced Bolívar to spend much of his time asserting his authority. It was not until 1818 that his political supremacy was assured, but even then the llaneros refused to operate outside their own provinces, and as a result Bolívar's attempt to recapture Caracas that summer failed.

The climax to the struggle for independence was nevertheless soon at hand. Bolívar knew that he had to give his supporters success and build momentum, yet the royalist forces were strong and held many reinforced positions in Venezuela. He therefore conceived of a bold and daring plan of immense risk. He opted to launch his campaign at the height of the *invierno* (the rainy season) when the rivers were swollen, plains flooded waist-deep and malaria was most prevalent. This would ensure that royalist troops, who would normally block his path, would have been withdrawn. But to achieve this Bolívar would be forced to cross the Andes in order to outflank the major garrisons, negotiating high passes choked with snow and ice. He would then have to use his pitifully small army of 2,500 men to fight greater numbers at the end of this epic march, and, under these circumstances, there could be no question of retreat. The odds against him were enormous.

The expedition began in June 1819, and, as expected, the crossing of the flooded plains proved arduous. The Arauca River provided the means to transport themselves for eight days by raft and canoe, although the journey was made miserable by unceasing rain. After disembarking, they discovered that the Plain of Casanare was flooded, which meant that the entire force had to wade waist-deep for miles. Heat, humidity and the constant wading through water made traversing the Llanos an exhausting venture, and sickness began to thin the ranks. Initially Bolívar's army had numbered just 2,400 men, with a few hundred women and followers carrying food and baggage – although they were later joined by a further 1,000 men. The weather stubbornly failed to improve, with thick fog or drenching rain throughout the march. In places the column was able to emerge from the water, but that in turn meant pushing through acres of thick mud. Parasites and leeches added to their burdens. Once Bolívar's men were clear of the plains, they began the long ascent of the Cordillera Oriental mountain range, eventually crossing the pass of Páramo de Pisba. Bolivar selected this pass as he believed it would be unguarded. However, with the highest point at 13,000 feet (4,000 metres) – well above the snowline – the arduous climb and deteriorating weather created new hardships for his little army. Some deserted, and one or two officers questioned Bolívar's judgment. Practically all the cavalry drifted away.

Cold and exhaustion also reduced the size of the company. Low temperatures, icy winds and blinding blizzards were the chief hazards, causing several men to die of exposure at night. Altitude sickness also depleted the ranks. The diet of dwindling rations was made more unappealing by the absence of wood for cooking. Bolivar nevertheless encouraged and urged the force on: the march had succeeded in giving him the element of surprise and he had no wish to squander the opportunity.

On 5 July, Bolívar's army emerged from the mountains and took the royalists by surprise. At the Battle of Vargas Swamp (25 July 1819) Bolívar ambushed a force trying to reach Bogotá, and at the Battle of Boyacá (7 August 1819) despite having lost a quarter of his initial little army, Bolívar compelled the royalists to surrender. The royalist government fled so precipitously that they left the entire treasury in Bolívar's hands, which greatly strengthened the republican cause. Bolívar consolidated his victory by uniting New Granada and Venezuela in the new state of Gran Colombia, and he agreed to a ceasefire with the royalists as a means to build up his army for the inevitable final struggle.

In 1821 the war was renewed, and Bolívar led an army of 7,000 men to victory at the Battle of Carabobo on 24 June 1821. This secured the north of the continent and allowed the Colombians to export their campaign for independence further south. To assist the republicans in taking the presidency of Quito, troops and supplies were dispatched under Antonio José de Sucre. The campaign was just as protracted and bitter as the ones before, and it was not until the following year, at the Battle of Pichincha on 24 May 1822, that Quito was secured. Peruvians, who had waged a long guerrilla war against the royalists, also looked to Bolívar and Sucre for support, but, while some rural areas fell to the patriots, the cities remained firmly in royalist hands until 1824. Finally, at the battles of Junín (in August) and Ayacucho (in December), the royalist armies were defeated, leaving only the upper highlands of Peru unconquered.

Further south, José de San Martín had led patriot forces successfully from 1817 in Chile, and had secured the entire country in just one year. While Bolívar had been assisted by dismissed British volunteers in his march across the Andes, a British naval officer, Thomas Cochrane, commanded the patriot navy in Chile. This fleet prevented any Spanish reinforcements reaching the beleaguered royal garrisons. Just as important was Rafael del Riego's revolt in Spain, which prevented the dispatch of any more military expeditions. The failure to augment the royalist armies prompted a wave of desertions or defections to the patriot cause. Thus, secure in the south, San Martin could use Cochrane's fleet to establish control of the waters off southern Peru. When negotiations with the Peruvian royalists broke down, he began to advance across the continent and captured Lima on 12 July 1821. Upper Peru, later renamed Bolivia in honour of *El Libertador*, surrendered in 1825, and all of the new independent states started to gain the recognition of the international community.

Bolívar, assisted by his allies, had succeeded in liberating an entire continent, despite years of setbacks. His inspiring leadership had, in effect, mobilized the peoples of South America against Spanish colonial rule. The support of Haiti and the popular backing of the Venezuelans and the rest of Gran Colombia had been crucial to the establishment of independence, but there can be no doubt that the campaign of 1819, which seemed doomed to failure, was the tipping point of the entire struggle. Despite the environment and the greater numbers ranged against them, Bolívar's small force had succeeded against all the odds.

5 /// THE WAR FOR
INDEPENDENCE, GREECE,
1821–29

*G*reece, along with the rest of the Balkans of southeast Europe, had fallen under Ottoman occupation when the Turks captured Constantinople in 1453. The Turkish empire also made a series of offensives deeper into central Europe and twice besieged Vienna. It was not until the late eighteenth and early nineteenth centuries that the European states could begin to push the Turks back, and it was not until the first decades of the twentieth century that the Ottomans were driven out of the Balkans.

Europeans came to regard the occupation of Greece with hostility for a number of reasons. During the eighteenth century, Greece and Macedonia were increasingly seen as the cradle of Western civilization, and some were bitter that such an important region languished under Muslim rulers. The Turks had, for example, built a small mosque within the ruins of the Parthenon, both the symbol of Athens' former glory, and, following its conversion to a church in the fifth century, a popular Christian site. After an accident involving gunpowder stored there during a Venetian bombardment, the Turks were also blamed for causing additional damage to the building. The Ottomans controlled many sites of religious significance in the Near East, including Jerusalem and Constantinople, however, the occupation of Constantinople was most significant for the Greeks. Not only had the city been the centre of the Byzantine empire (and therefore the last link with the Roman civilization held in such great esteem by the Europeans) but it was also the seat of the Christian Orthodox Church, and so particularly venerated by the Greeks. It was the clergy of Greece who preserved a sense of national identity, and furthermore their leadership of the Orthodox Church also provided an important conduit through which ideas could pass to the other Balkan peoples who belonged to the Orthodox denomination. A sense of separate identity was also fostered by the mistreatment of Greeks by Turkish governors. Although Greeks were able to develop their commerce and join the ranks of the administration, they were generally treated as second-class citizens or *rayas*. During periods of unrest Turkish irregulars earned a reputation for hideous reprisals, and all attempts at keeping order were immediately regarded with loathing by the Greek population. In 1770 Count Alexei Orlov mounted a Russian military expedition to liberate Greece, but its failure led to widespread repression, often by Albanian auxiliaries.

Previous pages. **Greek pirates. Painting by Carl von Heydeck, 1836.**

By the nineteenth century, Western European ideas of insurrection and liberty, kindled by the French Revolution and the Enlightenment, had spread across the continent. As Western Europeans rediscovered the classical Greek works, Greek scholars read of the inspiring virtues of constitutional governance – although intellectuals ran considerable risks if they attempted to disseminate these concepts. Rigas Feraios and his colleagues were executed in 1798 for advocating an independent Balkan Republic. Unwittingly the Turks themselves also contributed to the growth of Greek resistance by employing Christian auxiliaries (*Armatoloí*). These bands of fighters were recruited to combat the bandits (or *klephts*), of mainland Greece, though the relationship between the Armatoloi and the bandits was ambiguous. It was not unknown for local deals to be struck between them, not least because many impoverished rural communities relied on klepht raiders, or admired their long-standing defiance of the Turkish authorities. At times the Armatoloi were known to change sides in order to make greater financial gains, or to justify their continuing pay from the Turks. Armatoloi officers were also appointed to administer their own areas of operations, and by the time of the outbreak of the War for Independence they could, unaided by the Turkish rulers, provide trained military forces in Rumeli, Thessaly, southern Macedonia and Epirus. A more clandestine supporter of the independence struggle was the Philikí Etaireía (Friendly Society), a secret organization dedicated to liberation established in Russian Odessa in 1814. The society was founded by wealthy benefactors in Europe and America, and originally aimed to restore the Byzantine empire by seizing Constantinople, though the core of its supporters were Greeks with more modest aims.

The opportunity for revolt came in 1821, when the Turkish army was preoccupied with a war against Persia and the rebellion of a Turkish governor in Epirus. Under the guidance of Alexander Ypsilantis (a Greek officer in Russian service and leader of the Philikí Etaireía) uprisings were staged in Peloponnese districts, in the Danubian principalities and in Constantinople itself. Ypsilantis aimed to support the revolts by marching into the Danube Valley and calling upon the people of the Balkans to rise up and join him. Unfortunately Ypsilantis clashed with the Wallachian and Romanian leaders of the rising, and suffered the ignominy of being officially excommunicated by a cautious and conservative Orthodox clergy. The Russian foreign ministry, which disapproved of revolutionary movements across Europe, quickly disowned their officer too. Ypsilantis was soon isolated without his Romanian allies, and the Ottoman army moved to intercept him, finally crushing his battalion, 'The Sacred Band', at the Battle of Dragashani on 19 June 1821. Ypsilantis was forced to flee to Austria where he was imprisoned, and the Moldovan rebels who had supported the Balkan uprising were suppressed after a year of fighting.

In the Peloponnese, Ypsilantis' advance into the Danubian principalities was eagerly awaited, but there were significant divisions between those in favour of revolt and the more conservative senior clergy. Isolated attacks on Muslims in March 1821 indicated the general mood, even though the risks of a failed rebellion, namely harsh repression by the Turkish authorities, were understood by all. In Kalamata in Messenia, a force of 2,000 Maniot rebels gathered to strike against the Turkish garrison and the town was taken after four days of fighting. Settlements in Achaea were then taken over by the Greek rebels, and when the Turks launched a counter-attack from Patras on the northern coast of the Peloponnese they were driven back into their fortress. These early successes encouraged resistance elsewhere, and, by the end of the month, all the rural districts of the peninsula were in the hands of the revolutionaries. The Turks were nevertheless able to hold on to their fortresses in many of the ports, therefore retaining the opportunity to bring in reinforcements to take back the Peloponnese. The Greeks possessed no artillery to reduce the fortress walls and had to be content to lay siege, but this squandered the initiative. The provincial capital of Tripolitsa was the only landlocked garrison held by the Turks, and all their attempts to break the besieging ring there ended in failure. The Greeks contained them, and on 23 September the city fell to the rebels.

In Macedonia, Emmanouel Pappas, another member of the Philikí Etaireía, brought arms and ammunition secured from Constantinople to Mount Athos, where he planned to establish a base that could spread insurrection in support of Ypsilantis' expedition. The initial attempt by his forces to seize Turkish merchants' goods in Serres merely initiated reprisals by the Ottoman authorities. Some 400 civilians were taken hostage, including 100 monks from Macedonian monasteries, and the Turkish governor, Yusuf Bey, planned to capture more from Polygyros to ensure quiescence. When the villages of Polygyros and Chalkidiki rose in revolt, however, Yusuf Bey ordered the execution of his prisoners. This action so enraged the local population that more joined the revolt and attempts were made to sever communications between the Turkish forces at Thrace in the east, and those further south at Thessalonika. The Turks recovered and defeated the rebels at Rentina and then again more decisively at Kassandra. Pappas was forced to abandon his base area, and after further operations the Turks secured the surrender of the remaining rebel forces. Despite this, in central and western Macedonia the rebellion continued to flourish, not least because the Armatoloi joined the revolt and provided the military experience the rebels so desperately needed. General Mehmed Emin decided to march against this new threat with 10,000 regular Turkish troops and another 10,000 irregulars. Emin took Naousa in April 1822 after defeating determined resistance and punished the town's inhabitants brutally.

Revolts in central Greece spread from the southern provinces and several towns were captured. In April, the Greeks broke into Athens and drove the Turkish garrison onto the plateau of the Acropolis. By May, central Greece was in tumult and everywhere the Turks appeared to be losing control of the situation. Commander Omer Vrioni and his Turkish force managed to inflict two defeats on the rebels at Alamana and Eleftherohori, but he was checked at the Battle of Gravia (8 May 1821). Having marched to relieve the garrison at Athens, he evacuated Attica in September, leaving the region in Greek hands.

The Greek War for Independence inspired support from across Europe, but it was the willingness of the Greek people to endure a long campaign that exhausted the Turkish armies. A combination of foreign intervention and guerrilla warfare led to a political settlement.

Despite the creation of a national assembly, there was little coordination of the Greek forces. Having ejected the Ottomans, there seemed to be no overall strategy for the consolidation of their gains, and it was fortunate for them that the Turks were unable to bring sufficient strength to bear and destroy the rebellion. Crucially, Turkish logistical chains were vulnerable to attack by rebels, limiting the size of the forces that they could deploy, and the two main counter-offensives launched by the Turks were defeated at Dervenakia and Karpenisi. The rebellion thus continued to spread. Cypriot volunteers sailed to join the fighting on the Greek mainland and there was similar enthusiasm amongst the Cretans. The Turkish authorities believed the Orthodox clergy were the ringleaders, and executed those they suspected of supporting the revolt, though this only served to galvanize further resistance.

An unusual feature of the conflict was the Greeks use of a rebel fleet, which, despite the large size of the Turkish navy, enjoyed some successes. The aim was to disrupt the Ottoman supply and reinforcement routes from Asia Minor so as to cut off the Turkish garrisons entirely and make counter-offensives impossible. Each of the Greek islands possessed some light vessels upon which could be mounted small calibre guns, but there was no centralized command structure, and the Greeks had to rely on raiding techniques to escape the full might of the Ottoman battle fleets. The Turks could deploy more than 75 warships, all of which outgunned the Greek flotillas. To combat this overwhelming firepower, the Greeks employed fire ships, with the first successful attack being made at Eresos on 27 May 1821. This was followed by 59 further assaults, of which 39 succeeded. Greek captains showed remarkable courage in confronting the Turkish navy, and scored local successes off Patras and Spetses in the first months of the war.

But soon this courage would be tested further. The Sultan of Turkey had appealed to the Egyptians for military assistance in Crete, offering in return possession of the island in the future. On 28 May 1822, a fleet of 30 warships and 80 transports arrived with a 12,000-strong Egyptian expeditionary force, which soon swept through the Cretan hills, torching villages that showed any signs of resistance. When the Cretans tried to concentrate their forces, mustering 3,000 at Amourgelles on 23 August 1823, they were crippled by Egyptian artillery and overwhelmed by greater numbers. So far the Greeks had shown unity in the face of Ottoman opposition, however the rivalries of the various districts, factions and elites soon spilled over into conflict and in April and May 1824 a veritable civil war broke out. Even though funds were offered by the British to sustain the War for Independence, the arrival of the money seemed to deepen the rivalries and suspicions of the various factions.

In 1825, though the resistance in Crete appeared to have been crushed, a force of 300 returned from the mainland to start a guerrilla war. This succeeded in taking Gramvousa but was then contained. A similar attempt to restart resistance was made by Epirote Dalianis with 700 followers in 1828, but again, the Ottomans and their allies overwhelmed the smaller rebel band at Frangokastello and the entire Cretan resistance garrison was wiped out. The Egyptian intervention had provided the Ottomans with an opportunity to crush the Greeks elsewhere, and the divisions among the revolutionaries only seemed to increase the Turks' chances of success.

The Egyptians, led by Ibrahim Pasha, landed at Methoni on 24 February 1825 and soon mustered an army of 11,000 men. They quickly retook the island of Sphacteria, off Messenia, causing panic among the revolutionaries on the mainland. Next the Egyptians marched through the western Peloponnese, leaving a trail of destruction in their wake. By June, the Greeks had been defeated at Maniaki and Argos. At Messolonghi, where the British poet Byron died supporting the cause of independence, the Turkish army was able to mount its third siege attempt, which began in April 1825. The same month also saw the town of Navarino captured by an Egyptian force. The Greeks had not yet given up, however. A Greek flotilla managed to attack the Turks in the Gulf of Corinth and temporarily drove them off with fire ships. Fresh attempts were also made to relieve Messolonghi, and on 22 April the Greeks tried to cut a path through the Egypto-Turkish lines in order to carry away some 6,000 civilians by ship. Unbeknown to the rebels, a Bulgarian deserter had betrayed the mission and the Egyptians were waiting when the sortie materialized. Although almost 2,000 rebels managed to fight their way through, about 4,000 civilians were captured and enslaved. An attempt was made by the remaining garrison to blow themselves up with a gunpowder arsenal rather than be taken captive in this way.

Further south, Mani also held out despite Ottoman threats that a failure to capitulate would result in the town being stormed and all its inhabitants put to death. Not only did the Maniots remain defiant, they repulsed a major attack in

June 1826 and then managed to check subsequent offensives. A relief force from the central Peloponnese also provided some support for a time, however elsewhere, the overwhelming strength of Turkish and Egyptian forces was too great. Greek civilians were unable to prevent reprisals or offer much resistance. The revolt was in danger of complete collapse.

Foreign intervention appeared to be the only way to save the cause of Greek independence, but little seemed forthcoming. The Holy Alliance partners of Austria, Russia and Prussia continued to view the revolt with displeasure, and could not be seen to be encouraging this type of resistance lest it flourish against their own regimes at home. The Tsar himself did feel compelled to support the Orthodox Church, and he regarded the Turks as his enemies, not least because they controlled the Straits of Constantinople (the Bosphorus) – the strategic waterway to all the warm-water ports of the Black Sea. The British, by contrast, were unwilling to see the Turkish empire collapse, but, at the same time, they applauded the efforts of the Greeks to break free of Ottoman tyranny. By 1826, it was clear to the British that a negotiated settlement might avoid reprisals and disruption in the region and preserve peace between the European states. A delegation was sent to Russia to arrange a compromise and start mediation between the Greeks and the Turks under a joint Anglo-Russian supervision. Although the Greeks were willing to negotiate, the Turks and Egyptians believed themselves on the verge of victory and the Ottomans, therefore, stepped up their efforts to conclude the conflict by force.

When, in July 1827, news arrived that a fresh Egyptian naval expedition had left Alexandria for Navarino, British and French fleets were despatched to intercept it, and they were soon joined by the Russians. After a stand-off in which the Egyptians argued they were obeying their orders to crush the revolt, there appeared to be a compromise whereby the Western powers would prevent Greek raids if the Egyptians stopped their own offensive. Following a Greek surprise assault, however, the Egyptians moved out of Navarino to counter-attack, and the British felt compelled to act to prevent it. After skirmishes, a full-scale naval battle broke out, which resulted in the decimation of the Egyptian fleet. Only 14 of the original 89 ships survived the battle. The engagement prompted the Russians to declare war on Turkey, and France offered to send an army to clear the Peloponnese of Egyptian and Ottoman forces. The shift of power was not lost on the Greek rebels, who regrouped and marched on Athens. In Attica, the Greeks, fighting as a regular army for the first time, defeated a Turkish army at the Battle of Petra, marking the end of military operations in the region. The Turks conceded defeat and Greece was recognized as independent in 1830.

The Greek War for Independence had been a bitter struggle, scarred by massacres on both sides and protracted in its nature. Given the small size of the Greek forces and the sheer military power at the disposal of the Ottomans and the Egyptians, the success of the revolt is remarkable. Of course, one should acknowledge the importance of the terrain, which favoured guerrilla actions, and the significance of the intervention by foreign forces, but the Greeks had shown great resourcefulness and endurance. They had created a navy and an army from scratch, with limited funds or munitions, and sustained resistance for almost a decade. On several occasions their defeat seemed imminent, especially as they descended into faction-fighting in 1824, but their eventual victory acted as an inspiration to the peoples of the Balkans and was celebrated across Western Europe. It was essentially the first great rent in the rotting fabric of the Ottoman empire, and it was achieved against considerable odds.

6 /// THE BRITISH ARMY AT DELHI, INDIA, 1857

O utnumbered British forces, surrounded and deprived of logistical support
or hope of relief, fought on against determined Indian mutineers in 1857.
Although unable to trust their formerly loyal subjects, the British made
use of civilian and allied military personnel, especially the Gurkhas and
Sikhs, not only to withstand sieges such as Lucknow, but also to maintain a siege of
Delhi, even though the city was strongly held by far larger numbers of mutineers.
The climax of the campaign was marked by the relief of Lucknow and other canton-
ments, yet it was the assault on Delhi that, in spite of all the orthodox principles of
war, succeeded in breaking the back of the rebellion.

The outbreak of the mutiny, known in India as the First War of Independence
(many civilians rose up alongside the nation's troops), was sparked by the refusal of
sepoys from the Bengal Presidency army to accept a new rifle. They resisted because
its cartridges, which had to be bitten before use to release the gunpowder, were
greased in pig and cow fat. Since the former animal was considered unclean by
Muslims, and the latter sacred by Hindus, the greased cartridges were antagonistic
to both faiths. The first unit that refused to obey orders, the 3rd Bengal Cavalry,
was further angered by the subsequent punishment of 85 of their own *sowars* (troopers) and they rioted, killing their British officers. At Meerut, the seat of the mutiny,
the British believed the outbreak was isolated and could be contained, but it soon
became apparent that *fissad* (sedition) had infected much of the army. The mutineers marched off to Delhi, the capital of the old Mughal empire, to appeal to
Bahadur Shah II to be their leader and rouse the entire subcontinent against the
hated *feringhees* (foreigners).

At Delhi there were no British regiments, just three battalions of Bengal
infantry. On the morning of 11 May 1857, the mutineers arrived quite suddenly
and, despite the efforts of some British officers to close the entrances to the city,
the rebels secured the southern Rajghat Gate. Noisily proclaiming the hour of
deliverance, mobs of citizens saw an opportunity to loot and destroy the symbols
of British authority. British officers and their families were soon being cut down
and mutilated in the streets. At the palace, the chaplain and two girls were butchered. When some tried to seek refuge in the Main Guard, a bastion on the
northern walls, the sepoys of the garrison joined the mutineers and slaughtered

Previous pages: **The repulse of an assault on Delhi Ridge, 1857.**

them. A handful of British officers then summoned two field guns and some sepoys not yet involved in the fighting and recaptured the Main Guard in hand-to-hand fighting. The main magazine of the garrison, protected by nine British officers and troops of doubtful loyalty, was confronted by hundreds of angry mutineers who began to scale the walls. This gallant little band kept their assailants at bay for five hours, but then their ammunition ran out. They knew their fate was sealed but resolved that the ammunition and powder of the arsenal should not fall into the rebels' hands. Thereupon they decided to sacrifice themselves for the greater good. Lieutenant Willoughby set the fuse, and soon after the entire building was obliterated by a gigantic explosion. The detonation tore down neighbouring buildings and killed scores of rebels. Miraculously, six officers survived the blast and, in all the confusion, they escaped the city. At this stage of the battle the sepoys who had helped recapture the Main Guard now threw in their lot with the mutineers, and the surviving British soldiers and civilians were forced to flee – most making for the ridge to the northwest of the city. From there, telegraph officers sent urgent warnings to other garrisons about what had occurred.

Although the rebels outnumbered the British survivors, they made no move against them. Inside the city, the mutineers refused to cooperate with each other, and there was even disagreement over the execution of 52 European civilians who had been captured alive earlier in the day. Some of the rural population had joined the revolt, but others saw merely an opportunity to loot or extort from both sides and cared little for liberation or loyalty.

By 17 May, the British survivors of Delhi were joined by the garrisons of Ambala and Meerut and, under the command of General Barnard, this small contingent managed to wrest the Delhi Ridge from a larger force of mutineers at the Battle of Badli-ki-Serai. The ridge lay just three-quarters of a mile from the Kashmiri Gate of Delhi, with a canal to its west. The British built a series of redoubts along the crest, and the centre of the position, known as Hindu Rao's house, was occupied by the loyal Gurkhas of the Sirmoor Battalion. Unfortunately, the south of the ridge led into a maze of village streets and gardens, providing plenty of cover for the approach of their attackers. Through the days of May and June, more and more mutineers poured into the city from the south and east. From the ridge it was clear that Delhi was held too strongly for the British to even consider taking it by storm, unless they could muster greater numbers. It also became apparent that it was they who would be besieged, not the city of Delhi.

As early as 19 June, the mutineers made a major attack on the ridge, pushing in from three directions. The British and their allies were only just able to cling on and for a time contemplated evacuating the position altogether. Despite overwhelming odds, they fought on. Four days later the rebels tried again, and for a second time came within a hair's breadth of victory. The ridge was wreathed in smoke, with much of the fighting at close quarters. When the smoke cleared and the mutineers pulled back, bodies could be seen strewn across the ridge and its approaches. For days, these corpses putrefied and a serious risk of contamination and disease, especially cholera, added to the burdens on the exhausted British force. The heat grew intense and the only relief from the sun was the camp of flimsy tents erected behind the ridge, just out of reach of the cannon fire and buzzing musket balls. Periodic alarms from the picquets in front of the ridge roused the British to stave off another attack, but each clash caused their numbers to dwindle still further. In one week in July, 25 officers and 400 men were killed or wounded resisting raids. While rebels possessed 10 cavalry regiments, 15 infantry regiments and an unknown number of well-trained artillerymen, the British lamented their lack of siege guns and transport, the result of earlier cost-cutting measures in peacetime.

Hopes were raised by the arrival of the Corps of Guides, an elite Muslim formation 600 strong. To support the soldiers on the ridge, the unit's six companies of infantry and three troops of cavalry had braved the broiling sun and force-marched from the Punjab – travelling over 500 miles (800 km) in just three weeks. Soon after, Brigadier John Nicholson, a veteran of the Sikh Wars leading a force of 4,200 men and a siege train of guns, was within reach of the reinforced garrison. To prevent the British from mounting a bombardment with this new ordnance, the mutineers made a desperate sortie on 25 August at the height of the monsoon, but Nicholson had anticipated the move and routed the rebels at the Battle of Najafgarh. His technique was as much psychological as military: he had his guns open fire but ordered the infantry to march silently against the rebels until they were within just 110 yards (100 m), whereupon they delivered a single, devastating volley and then charged, bayonets levelled, with an indescribable war cry. The rebels bolted and most of the British force could concentrate on bayoneting and clubbing their way into a hastily built redoubt. The morale of the British on the ridge soared, but the mood among the rebels was one of bitterness and recrimination against their leaders.

The British redoubts were now filled with guns: 15 twenty-four-pounders, 20 eighteen-pounders and 25 mortars and howitzers, supported by 600 cartloads of ammunition. By stages, new batteries were constructed closer to the walls of Delhi. First, the rebels' guns on the Mori Bastion on the western wall were silenced, and this led the mutineers to believe that the British would assault from this direction. New batteries were built opposite the Kashmiri Gate and northern wall, with one (at the old Customs House) constructed just 220 yards (200 m) away. It didn't take long for the masonry and stonework to be smashed down, and a number of breaches appeared. Inside, the rebels were daily more disillusioned. One British officer wrote: 'guns and mortars were pouring shot and shell without a moment's interval on the doomed city. The din and roar were deafening; day and night salvos of artillery were heard, roll following roll in endless succession, and striking terror into the hearts of those who felt that the day of retribution was at hand.' Every effort to overwhelm the British had failed and now the rebels' own supplies of food and

The Indian Mutineers selected Delhi as their capital, but, despite their attempts to drive the British off the nearby ridge, they failed to take the initiative. British reinforcements counter-attacked the city and captured it after a desperate struggle.

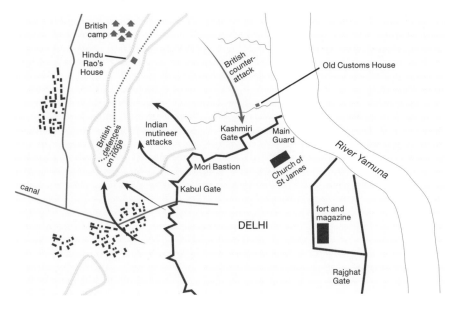

ammunition were reduced. Rumours of defeat were being spread by agents of the British inside the city. Despite their advantages, the assaulting British force was little more than 5,000 strong against many more thousands of rebels, both sepoys and citizens. The city itself was vast, and coordinating a major assault upon it was a significant challenge.

In the early hours of 14 September, it emerged that the mutineers had repaired some of the breaches during the night and so the attack on the city, planned for dawn, was rescheduled. The final assault was announced by a renewed British cannonade during the day, but the British had essentially lost the element of surprise. Now only hard fighting would decide the outcome. Two British columns each charged into a breach to open a savage struggle. The third column waited while two engineer officers, Lieutenants Home and Salkeld, rushed forward with gunpowder charges towards the Kashmiri Gate. Alerted to the direction of this attack, the mutineers tried to shoot down the two men as they set their explosives. It was a tense few minutes, but the charge detonated successfully and the third column fought its way through the debris into the city.

A fourth column, meanwhile, had attacked the Kabul Gate but was repulsed after initial success. It was bundled back so precipitously that the rebel counterattack threatened to retake the Delhi Ridge altogether. With the British forces battling away in the north of the city, only the reserve and the British cavalry could stem the rebels streaming out of the Kabul Gate. Neville Chamberlain, an officer badly wounded in an earlier battle, directed the battery at Hindu Rao's house from his stretcher. The British troops on the ridge were themselves pounded by rebel guns, including some of their own that had been captured in the withdrawal.

At the same time, in the city, their attack was also in danger of failure. Nicholson's own column was twice thrown back because rebel musketeers could both pour fire down into the streets from flat rooftops and windows, and fire grapeshot from doorways down the narrow alleyways. Nicholson himself led a third charge towards the Burn Bastion and was mortally wounded. Checked at this point, the column pulled back to the area around the Church of St James. General Archdale Wilson contemplated abandoning the attack altogether, but Nicholson, although dying, would hear none of it. For two days, the combat went on in and around the British bridgehead. Some rebel Muslim troops, calling themselves Mujahideen, wanted to fight to the death, but many of the rebels were dispirited by their losses and the sheer determination of their opponents to fight on. Gradually, the British managed to extend the area under their control. They retook the ruined magazine on 16 September and three days later recovered the palace. Bahadur Shah, the reluctant and inert leader of the revolt, had fled before they arrived, but he was captured by a detachment of cavalry soon after. Fearful that they might be trapped as the British took each bastion in turn, the majority of the rebels began to evacuate the city. On 21 September, after an epic battle lasting eight days, Delhi was back in British hands. Nicholson, satisfied, passed away two days later.

The force of British and loyal Indian troops had numbered 10,000, with Sikh, Gurkha and Pathan allies estimated at 3,000. In the final assault, over 5,700 of the British and their Indian allies had been killed or wounded. The casualty figures for the 42,000 rebels are unknown, but their losses may have been of a similar number. The stakes had been very high. The British knew that their ability to govern rested on breaking both the capability and the will of the rebel forces at India's former capital; indeed, the fall of Delhi proved a major psychological blow for the rebellion. By retaking the city, the British had signalled their determination to reassert exclusive rule. Angered by the massacre of British civilians, there were many who advocated a punitive regime, but, despite isolated atrocities, both the British and the Indians were eager to restore peace and order.

In the defence of the Delhi Ridge, the British and their allies had suffered from critical shortages of everything required for war. They had been depleted by disease, debilitated by heat and harried by frequent raids or more serious attacks, yet clung to their position with great resolve. It is a principle of war that a force should not make an attack on an enemy position without odds greater than three to one, but at Delhi, in the final assault, the British were outnumbered by that same ratio. While they possessed a superior armament of heavy guns and rifled muskets, this counted for little in the close-quarter fighting of the assault: the narrow streets and labyrinth of fighting positions actually conferred all the advantages on the defenders. In all, the defence of the Delhi Ridge and the retaking of the city should both have failed, and the actions of those men during the desperate months provide an inspirational reminder of resilience and endurance. The force at Delhi, despite all the odds against them, had not only recaptured a city, they had, in effect, achieved a strategic victory that enabled Britain to dominate India more comprehensively than ever before.

7 /// THE BATTLE OF BURNSIDE'S BRIDGE AT ANTIETAM, AMERICA, 1862

A t the Battle of Antietam, 17 September 1862, despite the sheer weight of firepower that Confederate infantry and artillery could muster against their Union opponents, the men of Burnside's Corps hurled themselves across an exposed stone bridge on the southern flank of McClellan's Union army. They gradually secured the crossing and then drove relentlessly on a narrow front onto the heights beyond. But for the late arrival of Confederate A. P. Hill's Corps on the field, Burnside's men, who were only engaged in a 'diversionary manoeuvre', came within an ace of winning the Maryland battle against the Confederate forces of Robert E. Lee.

The second autumn of the American Civil War marked the end of an ignominious period for the Union. Despite the high hopes of 1861, their forces had failed to crush the rebellion of the southern states, and in 1862 the Union effectively lost three Virginian campaigns in succession. In the Shenandoah Valley, despite a three-to-one numerical superiority, the Union troops had been outclassed by the manoeuvres of General 'Stonewall' Jackson and his Confederate infantry (nicknamed 'foot cavalry'). Soon after, Major General George McClellan led an army of 100,000 towards Richmond, the Confederate capital, but after a series of battles in the Seven Days' Campaign he was instead ordered to evacuate the Virginia Peninsula. Finally, Major General John Pope had also been deceived at the Battle of Second Manassas by Jackson and General Robert E. Lee, again despite superior numbers. In early September 1862, Washington, DC, was full of wounded or dispirited Union troops. McClellan was called upon to restore discipline and morale. For all his faults as a commander in the field, not least his excessive caution and procrastination, he did not lack the energy or enthusiasm for creating armies. In just four days, McClellan had reinforced and reorganized the Army of the Potomac to deploy seven corps of 90,000 men, with a further 70,000 in fortifications.

Unaware that the Federal army had been bolstered, Robert E. Lee decided to take the offensive. The plan was to feed his Confederate forces in northerners' fields, rather than in the impoverished south, and then to inflict a decisive defeat on the Union. This would force President Abraham Lincoln into a negotiated peace, and perhaps convince the states of Europe to intervene on the Confederates' behalf. Lee advanced quickly with five columns, but McClellan had reorganized so swiftly that

Previous pages: **The Battle of Antietam, 1862. Lithograph.**

he was actually marching to intercept him. Lee was also unaware that a copy of his plans had fallen into Union hands, meaning that McClellan was able to predict with some accuracy where each of the Confederate columns would be. His plan was to interdict them, defeating each one in turn.

Lee's forces had, however, fallen behind their march schedule, and Confederate cavalry patrols alerted Lee to the presence of the Union Army. Fighting a series of short, sharp actions in the uplands to the east of the Potomac River in Maryland, Lee withdrew his columns and concentrated in two locations: Harper's Ferry and Sharpsburg. He had with him just 18,000 men but was confident he would be joined by Jackson's reinforcements. Lee's flanks were anchored on the Potomac and his front was protected by the Antietam Creek. While his men were concealed in the folds of the rolling ground, farms, stone walls and woodland would offer cover.

When he arrived on 15 September, McClellan surveyed the Confederate position, but, despite having 75,000 men under his command, he was inclined to believe intelligence reports that suggested the army opposite numbered up to 100,000: a wildly exaggerated estimate. The arrival of Jackson's 9,000 Confederate troops on Lee's left the next day, coupled with field obstacles and the Confederate dispositions, gave an illusion of strength that did little to change this impression. In the centre of the Confederate position, Major General D. H. Hill's Division occupied a sunken lane as a natural entrenchment, and used wooden stakes to create a line of abbatis. On the right of Lee's line, Major General Longstreet's Corps, with the bulk of the Confederate artillery, was ordered to hold all the southern and eastern approaches, and this mass of men also reinforced the impression of a well-defended line.

When McClellan had finally decided to commence an attack at 1400 hours on 16 September, he ordered a preliminary bombardment from a number of his batteries, but the cannonade was far from effective. Consequently, he looked to make a flanking attack against Lee's left, while pushing Major General Ambrose Burnside's IX Corps in from the south. McClellan's cavalry and two corps were held in the centre to exploit the success of either flank. It took so long to get the various formations into place that little more than skirmishing occurred that day. Darkness and heavy rain interrupted any major action. To conceal their positions, McClellan ordered that no campfires be built and so the Union troops spent a miserable night in the soaking rain, knowing that, after dawn the next day, they would be thrown against the Confederate battle-lines. As dawn broke, Lee received a further reinforcement of 10,000 men, bringing his total strength to 37,000.

The battle recommenced at 0600 hours, with Union guns pounding the Confederate lines. As the main Federal attack got underway in the north near Dunker's church, the Union artillery played havoc with Confederate infantry stationed in a cornfield and swept them away. The offensive seemed to be going well, and the Union troops marched in pursuit as the survivors of the original Confederate line fell back, but moments later Jackson's men appeared and their dauntless counter-attack soon had the tired and astonished Union troops reeling back across the ground they had won. Each of the Confederate regiments, however, tended to push too far, and once again Union artillery cut them down in swathes. At this juncture, a new Union corps, the XII, threw the Confederates back, but, just as it advanced, it too was cut to pieces. Inexperienced soldiers broke and ran, while hundreds more were pinned down near Dunker's church, unable to get forward or withdraw without suffering terrible losses.

On the Confederate side, losses were just as stunning. Captains took command of shattered brigades, and some regiments were reduced to a handful of unwounded troops. Yet, miraculously, when the fresh Union II Corps started to march up and cross the Antietam Creek, Jackson's exhausted men rallied and took what cover they could find to pour fire into the oncoming Union masses. The arrival of some Confederate brigades previously held in reserve on the flank of the Union advance meant that the Federal soldiers suddenly found themselves in a crossfire; in twenty minutes 5,000 were killed and wounded, and several units disintegrated entirely.

Despite this, elements of II Corps pressed on towards the Confederate centre where Hill's Division were manning the sunken lane. The Union troops advanced with parade-ground precision, and were allowed to come to within short range before the Confederates unleashed their first volley. The Union troops seemed to hesitate only briefly and then resumed their advance. Each subsequent volley produced a similar effect. A Confederate counter-attack at this point broke through the Union line but was itself stopped short by the Union Irish Brigade. This formation of immigrants from New York hurled the Confederates back, straddled the sunken road and poured fire along it, cutting down defenders. The sunken road was soon so choked with dead and dying men that it was later given the epithet 'bloody lane'.

The Union attack might have pressed on right through the collapsing centre of the Confederates' lines, but fatigue, the last-ditch resistance of the survivors and the arrival of Lee's final reserves halted the northerners' advance. As McClellan pondered throwing his remaining troops against the fragile Confederate defences, he was advised by his corps commanders that their lines had been decimated. Major General Fitz-John Porter, commanding V Corps, pointedly remarked: 'Remember, General, that I command the last reserve of the Republic.' McClellan paused and then called off the attack in the centre. He could not have known just how close he had come to victory, but his inherent caution and the advice of his comrades made the decision for him.

The stone bridge across the Antietam Creek in the southern portion of the battlefield was one of those features that seems to assume an importance out of all proportion to its size, and creates an effect of tunnel vision on military leaders. On either side of the bridge, the waist-deep river could be forded, while the narrow span of the bridge – which was just 12 feet (4 m) wide – canalized troops, turning even small numbers of men into a mass that was an easy target for the Confederates dug in on the steeply wooded slopes that lay to the west. Burnside had been ordered south to make a diversionary manoeuvre to support the Union thrusts further north earlier that day, but he had also been instructed to await further orders, and had done so until about 1000 hours. By then, the Confederates had stripped out all available men until just 2,000 remained to watch over the bridge and stream, against 11,000 of Burnside's IX Corps and 50 guns. In fact, opposite the bridge itself, the Confederates had just 600 men, but they were well entrenched and could dominate not just the bridge but also its approach road, with 12 cannon in place to blast any assault force with round shot and, at close quarters, canister.

When he was finally ordered forward, Burnside decided to send a reinforced division further south to cross at a less well-defended point. This division would then return northwards and clear the Confederate positions from the flank. The Kanawha Division, led by Brigadier General Jacob D. Cox (who also held nominal command of the corps on Burnside's insistence), was tasked with attacking across the bridge in a direct assault at the same time. At the head of the assault force was the 11th Connecticut, led by Henry Kingsbury, a 25-year-old colonel who was highly popular with his men.

Kingsbury assembled his troops behind a low hill just 200 yards (180 m) from the bridge, and then, on his signal, they rushed forward. Within seconds, withering fire was cutting down these Union skirmishers. Only one company managed to reach the stonework of the bridge. Another plunged into the creek, as bullets ripped up the surface around them. Captain Griswold, their leader, was one of the few to actually get across the stream, only to fall wounded on the far bank. Kingsbury, urging his dwindling command forward, was hit four times and fell mortally wounded. A brigade that tried to follow the Connecticut attack lost their direction and ended up some hundreds of yards to the north of the bridge, and they failed to get across the water at all. Finally a brigade that was assembled on the road ready to make a densely packed charge down to the bridge suffered such heavy losses from Confederate sharpshooters that they were soon pinned down. Those Union survivors who were able melted back to the cover of the hill, having lost a third of their strength in less than 15 minutes of fighting.

By midday, McClellan had ordered that Burnside should make a full assault rather than a diversionary action, and in his exasperation demanded success even if it cost the lives of ten thousand men. Burnside ordered up one more brigade and decided that the vanguard of this new attack was to be made by the

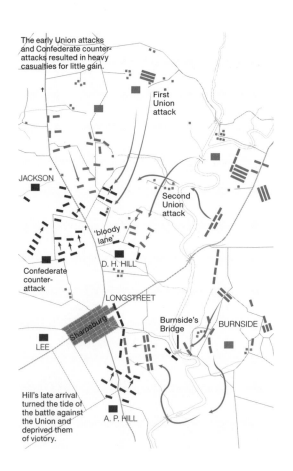

The early Union attacks and Confederate counterattacks resulted in heavy casualties for little gain.

First Union attack

JACKSON

Second Union attack

'bloody lane'

D. H. HILL

Confederate counterattack

LONGSTREET

Sharosburg

Burnside's Bridge

BURNSIDE

LEE

Hill's late arrival turned the tide of the battle against the Union and deprived them of victory.

A. P. HILL

In a bloody and inconclusive battle, two of Burnside's regiments exhibited extraordinary courage under fire and secured a river crossing that, but for the arrival of Confederate reinforcements, would have given the Union Army a decisive victory.

51st Pennsylvania and 51st New York, regiments with good fighting reputations. To aid this renewed assault, Union artillerymen manhandled their guns to the flanks and began strafing the Confederates with canister. If this suppressive fire was supposed to save the assaulting troops, it failed. Within minutes of coming into view of the bridge, the Union infantrymen were dropping in their ranks. The formation broke up and the troops ran forward to try, vainly, to find some cover by the bridge itself. The Pennsylvanians were to the right and some took shelter behind a stone wall, but the New Yorkers, with no cover but a rail fence, were left exposed to the fire of the Confederates entrenched just 25 yards (23 m) distant. For a few minutes, both sides blazed away as fast as they could. Minié balls were splintering the tree trunks and fences, ricocheting from the stonework of the bridge, or crashing into men's flesh. Lieutenant George Whitman, Union officer and brother of the poet Walt Whitman, wrote that he and his men 'showered lead' across the creek. Canister cases exploded from the muzzles of nearby cannon, adding to the blizzard of fire sweeping the space between these two lines of men. The dead and dying lay strewn between, and the wounded tried hopelessly to crawl away, searching for some cover.

Anxiously, Burnside's officers looked to the south, hoping the division sent to cross further downstream would return and attack the Confederates' right flank. No one appeared: the division had found the designated crossing point unsuitable and had been forced to march further away from the fighting. If the bridge was to be carried at all, it had to be done by the Pennsylvanians and New Yorkers themselves.

The intensity of fire had not slackened for an instant. The crack, buzz and sickening thump of bullets finding their mark had gone on for a full 30 minutes, and soon the Confederate soldiers in the front line realized that they were down to their last few cartridges. On the Union side of the river, the situation seemed to be just as bleak. Ammunition pouches were almost empty and there was no chance of getting more across the exposed and fire-swept space behind them.

Then, in that instant, something extraordinary happened. Captain William Allebaugh stood up and dashed forward onto the bridge itself. Behind him came the first sergeant, two colour-bearers and, on their heels, the colour guard with bayonets fixed. The sight of the two colours billowing over the span inspired the Union men and they rose as one to race across the stonework. Soon the entire bridge was filled with charging Federal troops. The Confederate soldiers fired off their final volleys, bringing down more men, but now the blue tide was irresistible: the New Yorkers and Pennsylvanians had been seized by the sheer exhilaration of their own momentum. The Confederates rushed back up their wooded slopes, retreating towards the town of Sharpsburg. The bridge had been carried.

The assault had cost the lives of 500 Union men, while the Confederates left 160 dead on the opposite slopes. As the assault wave crested the first ridge, in a moment of irony, the Union flanking division came into view on their left. More regiments now piled in behind, their shoes marching through the blood of their comrades and raising columns of dust. McClellan was aware that Burnside's success offered the chance to defeat Lee even though all the other assaults had been checked. This would, however, mean getting several divisions, artillery, ammunition wagons and staff across the narrow bridge. Estimates indicated this would take at least three hours, and Lee was alert to the threat Burnside now posed. While the Union tried to resupply its exhausted assault troops with ammunition and reinforce the bridgehead, Lee used the time to concentrate his artillery, including Parker's battery, which was made up of young men aged between 14 and 17 (an indication of manpower shortages in the Confederate army). Lee then received word that General A. P. Hill's Light Division had marched non stop to reach the battlefield, and these crucial reserves might be enough to turn the tide in his favour.

Burnside had also been energetic; his entire IX Corps had assembled on the far bank of the Antietam by 1500 hours, just two hours after the bridge had been taken. Of these, 8,000 men and 22 guns were ready to push on to Sharpsburg and crush Lee. One observer wrote that: 'the earth seemed to tremble beneath their tread'. The Confederates poured desperate fire into them and the arrival of Hill's Division at the critical moment caused the Union advance to at first stall, and then to give ground. Some of Hill's men were carrying Union colours taken as trophies from a depot at Harper's Ferry and some wore uniforms of a similar blue to the Union army, causing confusion among the troops. As the Union attack broke up, so the Confederate force that had marched or fought all day, also reached the point of exhaustion. Burnside's men sheltered as best they could just to the west of the creek, with the bridge at their back. The Confederates tried to find cover in the woods and folds of the ground south of Sharpsburg. As darkness fell, the troops expected to renew the bloody encounter in the morning, but the leaders on both sides had learnt that a tactical defence was more economical in terms of lives. Lee took the initiative and decided to slip away, back to the south. Fearing another deception or a counter-offensive, McClellan accepted the advice of those who urged him to stay put.

Burnside's corps had suffered losses amounting to 20 per cent of their original strength, but they had opened up a crucial flank against Lee and forced him to commit his final reserve. Had McClellan renewed the offensive with the fresh divisions at his disposal, historians agree that he could have defeated Lee. However, this, the bloodiest battle of the entire Civil War, seemed to have sobered all levels of command. It is estimated that, in a single day's action, the Union had lost 12,500 men and the Confederates 10,000. The nature of the fighting around Burnside's Bridge seemed to characterize the entire battle, and the incredible courage of the combatants, particularly the 51st Pennsylvanians, and 51st New Yorkers, was a remarkable success of human will against the sheer firepower of modern weaponry.

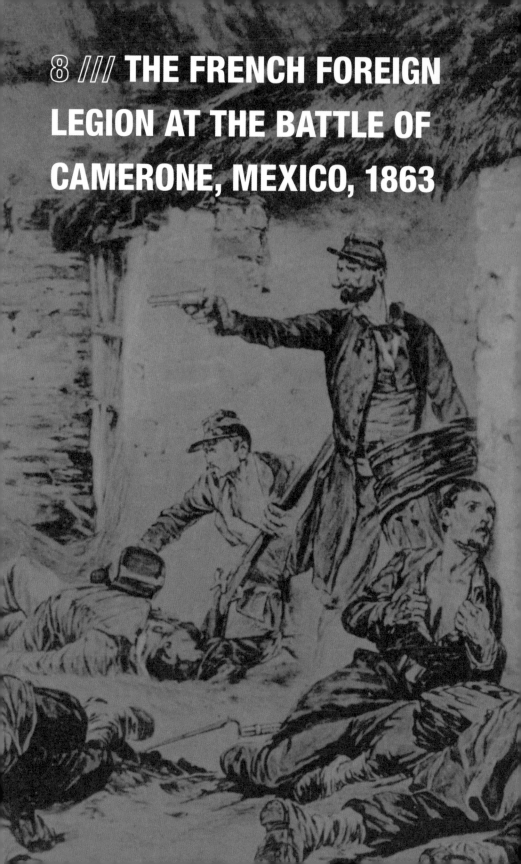

8 /// THE FRENCH FOREIGN LEGION AT THE BATTLE OF CAMERONE, MEXICO, 1863

T he last stand of an isolated detachment of the French Foreign Legion in Mexico came to represent the spirit of that illustrious unit. Their self-sacrifice epitomized the sense of duty and honour that superseded all other considerations, including survival, and symbolized the determined ethos of the Legion.

The French military intervention in Mexico, subsequently known as the Franco-Mexican War, had been provoked by the Mexican government defaulting on interest repayments in July 1861. The fleets of Great Britain, Spain and France arrived at Veracruz soon after, with the intention of pressuring the republican government of Benito Juárez into submission. Though some Spanish troops had been dispatched, it was neither the intent of Britain nor Spain to launch a full military expedition. It was the arrival of the French army and their occupation of the eastern city of Campeche on 27 February 1862 that demonstrated the French were far more belligerent than their other European partners. Concerned that France intended to establish a permanent occupation, the British and Spanish withdrew their forces.

Napoleon III, Emperor of the French, believed the situation in Mexico offered him a number of benefits. He was eager to demonstrate the military power of the French empire and thereby to establish a more favourable diplomatic position in Europe. He was also keen to re-establish good relations with the Austrian Habsburg empire after an inconclusive and costly war against them in 1859, as such diplomacy would be the means to link the crowned heads of Europe and suppress republican or revolutionary movements. Action against the secular republic of Mexico in favour of a Catholic restoration and a rapprochement with Austria would also please Napoleon's Roman Catholic supporters at home. In April 1862, however, the Mexican government remained defiant, and a blockade of the Pacific port of Mazatlán failed to change the situation. Indeed, the check of a French force at the Battle of Puebla (5 May 1862), at the hands of the Mexican forces under General Ignacio Zaragoza, indicated the need for a stronger effort. The Mexican army was halted outside the city of Veracruz at Orizba on 14 June, and French reinforcements began to arrive in September (rising to a total of 38,400 troops by the end of the year). Through October, General Achille Bazaine repeatedly took the offensive,

Previous pages: **Battle of Camerone in Mexico, 1863.**

capturing Tampico, Tamaulipas and Xalapa, and then, after a bombardment on 15 January 1863, securing Veracruz.

The next objective of the French expeditionary force was Puebla, and, in March 1863, General Élie Frédéric Forey was tasked to lay siege to the city. The Mexicans could muster a total of 80,000 men but most of these forces were dispersed in garrisons. It was still possible, however, to dispatch relatively small formations to harass the French and try to cut their lines of communications from the coast. The French besieging force at Puebla had requested stocks of food, ammunition and tools, as well as three million francs. These supplies had to be transported with a relatively small guard along an obvious route: factors that played into the Mexican army's hands.

The protection of the convoy was the responsibility of Captain Jean Danjou, who was assisted by Lieutenants Clément Maudet and Jean Vilain, and accompanied by 62 Legionnaires of the 3rd Company, Légion étrangère (French Foreign Legion). Danjou was a veteran with considerable military experience. He had served in Algeria where, during a close-quarter battle, his rifle had exploded and so damaged his hand that it had to be amputated. Despite the injury, Danjou went on to serve in the Crimean War at the Siege of Sebastopol, and then at the battles of Magenta and Solferino in northern Italy during the Franco-Austrian War (1859). When he received orders to assist in the protection of a supply column of carts and mules, he lost no time in assuming command of a small detachment of Legionnaires. Dressed in their characteristic blue jackets, baggy red pantaloons and white kepis, they each carried a rifled musket with its long bayonet and laboured under the weight of a heavy pack. The force was, as everyone later agreed, far too small for the task, but sickness had reduced the number of available troops and the dashing Danjou was forced to press the only men he had left into service.

This small detachment had marched through the night to avoid the heat of the day, and at 0700 hours on 30 April, they halted to rest. Before they had even had the opportunity to brew coffee, several squadrons of Mexican cavalry appeared, and the Legionnaires had to scramble into a square formation – still the traditional way to resist attacks by horsemen despite the introduction of longer-range rifled weapons in the French army. The Mexican cavalry nevertheless believed that their superior numbers and the element of surprise gave them a

French troops established the regime of Emperor Maximilian, but Mexican resistance increased steadily. The interception of a French Foreign Legion detachment at Camerone led to a short, but epic, battle.

distinct advantage and charged. For some time, the French Legionnaires held their position, inflicting a number of casualties on the Mexicans and driving off several spirited charges. Despite this, Danjou was aware that his position was too exposed and the densely packed ranks were too large a target. He therefore ordered that, while maintaining a loose square, the Legionnaires were to withdraw towards a hacienda near by. They did so, taking casualties along the way. Hacienda Camerone was a rough adobe-and-wood structure, but it possessed a 10-foot (3-m) high mud wall that would at least offer some protection against cavalry. Danjou's aim was to hamper the Mexican cavalry long enough for the convoy to escape. While some of the Mexican cavalry dismounted to engage the French, Danjou had at least survived the initial onslaught.

The French position was critical. The Mexican cavalry had prevented Danjou entering the village of Camerone, and even the main structure of the hacienda had fallen into their hands. Confined to a compound around which stood some ruined outbuildings, the position was hardly tenable. Mexican sharpshooters accounted for some Legionnaires who were trying to cover the gaps in the

//

walls, but the French did manage to beat off the rushes of dismounted troopers and the mounted charges.

Colonel Francisco de Paula Milan, the commander of the Mexican cavalry, believed that the foreigners had no options left. He called on the French to surrender, but Danjou was still hoping to buy time and refused. It is alleged that the French captain also swore he would fight to the death and that his Legionnaires, inspired by this determination, expressed the same sentiment. Their situation began to change at 1100 hours when Milan's reinforcements, a battalion of 1,200 infantrymen, arrived. The hacienda was soon encircled and fire began to pour in. Outnumbered twenty to one, the Legionnaires were exposed to the cruel heat of the sun, had no water, and had only the ammunition that each man carried in his pouches. For over an hour shots were exchanged, with casualties mounting steadily on both sides. The hacienda caught fire, the smoke and flames adding to the miseries of the dwindling garrison. By midday, half of the French force was either dead or wounded. Then, suddenly, Danjou himself was hit full in the chest. He died instantly.

Under cover of fire, the Mexican infantry tried to edge forward, and for a further four hours the French detachment maintained their fusillade. It was a very one-sided affair. Vilain was killed towards the end of the afternoon, leaving Maudet and just 12 others to continue the resistance. Surrounded by the dead and dying, and wreathed in smoke by the smouldering ruins of the hacienda, this tiny force was unable to cover the entire perimeter. The Mexicans were now able to bring fire to bear on every part of the position, and at around 1700 hours, after a day of fighting, only Maudet and five Legionnaires remained.

With all their ammunition expended, Maudet and his men decided to launch a desperate bayonet charge in order to take as many Mexicans with them as possible. It was a hopeless but courageous gesture. As they emerged from the ruined hacienda, the fire intensified. Two were killed instantly but the others raced forward. As the bullets cracked around them, Legionnaire Catteau tried to shield the lieutenant with his own body, but he was shot down and Maudet fell seconds later. The two survivors, both shot and wounded, lay exhausted and resigned to death, but the Mexican commander ordered a ceasefire. He offered them the chance to surrender, and, defiant to the end, they would agree only if they were permitted to keep their rifles and escort the other wounded, and the body of Captain Danjou, back to the coast. Somewhat astonished, but touched by their devotion to duty and to their fallen leader, Milan agreed. It is claimed he muttered to his own troops: 'What can I refuse to such men? No, these are not men, they are devils.'

Thanks to the unquestionable heroism of Danjou and his men, the convoy did indeed make its way intact to the French forces besieging Puebla, and seventeen days later the city fell. General Bazaine defeated the Mexican relieving force at the Battle of San Lorenzo (8 May 1863) and then went on to enter Mexico City in June that year. The Mexican government fled to the north to continue its resistance from there, but more and more of the country fell under French control. On Napoleon III's prompting, the Habsburg dynasty provided the new ruler, Emperor Maximilian I of Mexico, in April 1864. An Imperial Mexican army was created, with Austrian volunteers augmenting the new force. Republican Mexican resistance continued, however, into 1865, and the United States, emerging from four years of Civil War, demanded that the French occupation be brought to an end. Some 50,000 US troops assembled on the Rio Grande and, fearing a war with America, the French began to evacuate Mexico in February 1866. Maximilian's forces were subsequently defeated by Mexican republicans in a series of battles until, in 1867, the capital fell back under the control of Juárez. Maximilian, accused of having ordered the execution of all rebels who opposed him, was shot by firing squad in June that year, and the republicans were restored to government.

The French Foreign Legion, which had suffered the bulk of the casualties of the French expeditionary force in the war, was eager not to lose sight of the achievement of Danjou and his detachment at Camerone. Some time after the battle, Danjou's prosthetic hand was found on the site of the fighting. He had worn the wooden limb painted as a glove, but somehow it must have been ripped from his body in the confusion of battle and been left behind. It was restored to the Legion some years later and on Camerone Day the wooden hand is still paraded. The Legionnaires also drink a ceremonial coffee to remember the fact that Danjou's men were denied this small privilege on the morning of 30 April 1863. The battle honour 'Camerone', embroidered on the flag of the Légion étrangère, is held in particular esteem by the Foreign Legion. The epitaph erected at the site of the battle, but since lost, recorded that: 'They were less than sixty opposed to a whole army. Its mass crushed them. Life rather than bravery gave up these French soldiers at Camerone on 30 April 1863.' Even if one allows for a certain license in this text, Danjou and his Legionnaires had exhibited an exceptional courage, and, more for the sake of honour than any tactical reason, they had fought on against all the odds.

9 /// LORD ROBERTS AND THE MARCH FROM KABUL TO KANDAHAR, AFGHANISTAN, 1879–80

*T*he Amir of Afghanistan, Sher Ali Khan, faced an impossible dilemma. On opposite sides of his troublesome realm lay the Russian and British empires, which were rivals in trade, in the establishment of colonies and influence in Asia. Britain regarded Afghanistan as a buffer state between the sprawling Russian dominions of central Asia and its own possessions in India, and viewed any interference with Afghanistan as the prelude to a Russian thrust towards the subcontinent. To counter that threat, Britain deployed agents and consuls, made strong signals to Tsar Alexander of Russia and, where necessary, deployed military forces to reinforce its claims. The Russians were aware that, despite the size of their empire and its vast reserves of manpower, they were financially weak and constantly threatened with internal unrest, perhaps even revolution. They regarded it as essential to maintain the prestige of the Tsar and to put pressure on foreign rivals with a show of force whenever the empire seemed to be threatened.

From 1877 to 1878, Russia was embroiled in a war with the Ottoman Turks and the campaign in the Balkans had been protracted. When the Russians had finally broken through the Turkish defences at Plevna in Bulgaria, and seemed poised to capture Constantinople, Britain dispatched a fleet to the Dardanelles, assembled a force of domestic and Indian troops at Malta and threatened war in response. In the Russian capital, the Ministry of War believed the only way to counterbalance the British threat was to send an army through the wastes of central Asia, promising the Afghans plunder from the plains of India. Colonel Nikolai Stoletov was sent ahead of the army to start a diplomatic offensive to ensure the safe passage of the Russian force.

British agents alerted the government of India – under the viceroyalty of Lord Lytton – to the Russian envoy, and the British rulers in Calcutta demanded that the Afghans receive a diplomatic mission to maintain their interests and to counteract the Russian move. Although the British had no knowledge that a tsarist army was approaching, Lytton was suspicious about both the Russian and Afghan motives, particularly when his demands for a mission were turned down by the Amir. Lytton sent an ultimatum, but still the Afghans refused to negotiate. If the Amir felt that hosting the Russian envoy meant that he would enjoy the backing of

Previous pages: **British and Indian troops at Kabul, making ready to repel attack by the Ghazis, 23 December 1879.**

the Tsar's soldiers when they arrived, he was to be bitterly disappointed: Britain and Russia managed to avert a war in the Balkans, and the Russians abandoned their march towards India. Just as Stoletov's mission withdrew, the British ultimatum expired and the fortress of Ali Masjid at the head of the Khyber Pass was captured by British and Indian troops.

The regular Afghan army was in no position to defeat the British, and after a couple of engagements, the most serious at Peiwar Kotal, the way to Kabul was open. Sher Ali had fled and died north of the Hindu Kush, and his son, Yakub Khan, was in no mood to fight the British. In May 1879, the new Amir was compelled to sign a treaty at Gandamak that gave the British control of his foreign affairs and forced him to accept a permanent British resident in the capital. The war appeared to be over and the British troops withdrew. Within weeks, however, the new Residency had been attacked by mobs of mutinous Afghan soldiers. Stationed there was a small detachment of the elite Corps of Guides, led by Major Sir Louis Cavagnari (the British Resident in Kabul) and Lieutenant W. R. P. Hamilton. They refused to surrender and fought on without hope of relief. The Residency was set alight, and part of the building had to be abandoned. The Afghan assailants were also able to use the cover of narrow streets and neighbouring buildings to get close to the windows. Eventually, the defenders had to fight from the first floor. To clear the approaches and to neutralize a cannon that had been brought up to blast the walls, Hamilton and 25 others made three charges out of the building, each one clearing the street only temporarily. With the British officers dead or dying, the Afghans appealed to the Muslim soldiers still alive inside to surrender, but the Guides refused to betray their regiment. A fourth sortie was made but its success was again short-lived. The gates were forced, the fire caused part of the building to collapse and the Afghans rushed in. The remaining troops fought to the last man – with Hamilton's actions earning him the first posthumously awarded Victoria Cross – but they were all cut down. Their bodies were mutilated, and their remains tossed onto the city's rubbish heap while the ruins of the Residency were looted for anything of value.

When Major General Sir Frederick Roberts, the commander of the Kabul Field Force, heard of the massacre, he immediately halted the withdrawal that was underway and force-marched his way back to Kabul with 6,500 men. Amir Yakub Khan, afraid of the city mobs, was offered protection by Lord Roberts, but the reluctant leader quickly abdicated, saying he would 'rather be a grass-cutter in India' than remain on the throne in Afghanistan. Roberts therefore found himself the de facto governor of the country, and, while the government in India wondered who could replace the Amir, Roberts tried to establish who had been responsible for the massacre of the British Resident and his escort. A number of former Afghan soldiers were captured and Roberts organized a military tribunal, which sentenced the ringleaders to be executed by hanging. At the same time he was careful to win over the people of Kabul by ensuring public order and opening a health clinic. For some weeks these measures proved successful, but the Afghans were concerned that the British might intend to stay as permanent occupiers. As the autumn drew on, individual tribes clashed with British outposts. Gradually the resistance strengthened, and by December a large coordinated insurgency had evolved. Tribal leaders tried to concentrate their vast numbers of irregular fighters on the capital, and the number of skirmishes increased dramatically. Eventually, tens of thousands of fighters occupied the hills around the capital. Roberts withdrew his garrison into an entrenched camp at Sherpur to await the onslaught.

The Afghans' attack began on 15 December, and lasted several days, gradually closing in around the British cantonment. Preparations were made for a final night assault on 23 December that would overrun the foreign infidels and result in a massacre of the garrison. Mullahs inculcated a militant religious fervour and the fighters encouraged each other. As the hour of the attack approached, scaling ladders were assembled and the great mass of tribesmen crunched softly through the snow towards the walls. But Roberts had received intelligence warning him of the precise hour of the attack. His men were stood to arms, field guns loaded and bayonets fixed. Although his forces were stretched thin by the length of the perimeter, a few star shells lit up the advancing Afghans and allowed Roberts to concentrate and direct his firepower. As the first explosions burst among them, the Afghans drew their long knives, fired their rifles and muskets wildly at the walls, and then broke into a run. The British and Indian troops waited until the Afghans presented the best possible target, then opened fire. Breech-loaders could be aimed and shot several times a minute, and with the order 'rapid fire', up to 15 aimed shots could be unleashed by each rifleman. The effect was devastating, and by 1300 hours the following day the Afghan attack had been smashed. As the tribesmen tried to escape they were set upon by cavalry armed with lances and swords, adding further

///

casualties to the toll. The revolt at Kabul had been broken up and once again the country seemed secure.

Away to the south, however, the situation was soon rather different. On 27 July 1880, Major-General James Primrose, the commander at Kandahar, had sent a brigade out to Maiwand to locate and destroy an Afghan army reportedly led by a new pretender to the throne, Ayub Khan. The combined British and Indian field force numbered 2,476 but its reconnaissance failed to locate any enemy forces. Turning to the north, they suddenly found themselves confronted by Ayub Khan's army in a great semicircular arc and were subjected to a fierce cannonade. Lingering on the flanks of the Afghan host were thousands of tribesmen who began to edge their way around the hastily formed British army firing line. Broken terrain offered the Afghans considerable cover, and after some hours – and very heavy losses – the Indian troops on the left of the British line were in danger of envelopment. The Afghans then sprang their main attack, engulfing the smaller British force. Small knots of men tried to stem the tide, and the 66th formed a ragged square to fight it out to the last man. In a matter of hours, 934 British and Indian soldiers lay dead, and a further 175 were missing. Wounded men were butchered, and any isolated parties trying to carry away

The defeat of a small brigade at Maiwand and the siege of Kandahar prompted a gruelling relief march by General Roberts. On arrival, they flew straight into battle and defeated the Afghans under Ayub Khan.

their injured colleagues were likewise surrounded and cut down. Fugitives trickled back into Kandahar but the 4,000-strong garrison was depleted and demoralized by the defeat at Maiwand and seriously outgunned and outnumbered. During the early part of August Ayub Khan moved his army to within range of the city and decided to lay siege.

Roberts was given command of a flying column that would march to the relief of Kandahar as soon as possible. He set out on 9 August 1880, reasoning that the Kandahar garrison could not wait until more British forces came up from India through the Bolan Pass. Roberts would have to cut himself from the supply routes that ran from Kabul to reach the beleaguered force in time. The route to Kandahar meant a march of over 90 miles (145 km) through some inhospitable terrain. Moreover, the broken ground forced Roberts to leave his field guns behind and take only light mountain artillery. To add to the challenge, the march would have to take place at the hottest time of the year, and it was likely that swarms of tribesmen would harass the column. Orders were issued that no man was to be left behind, and vigilance in security was to be strictly maintained. Despite this, the 9,986 fighting men, 8,000 followers and 10,000 transport animals (including ponies, mules and camels) were strung out for five miles, even where the terrain permitted a fairly cohesive formation. Roberts therefore organized his force in three brigades, each part able to support the other. Cavalry were thrown out front and rear and on either flank to act as a screen for the main force, but their patrol pattern meant that they daily had to march and ride greater distances than the main body of the column, adding to their fatigue.

Roberts had been meticulous in his planning and provisioning. Private Samuel Crompton of the 9th Lancers recalled that 'So perfect was the foresight of our chief that, when at last we got to Kandahar, we had three days' supplies in hand.' Crompton also remarked on the sights and sounds of 'grumbling camels, the stubborn donkeys, the wild little native ponies and the patient, plodding horses' and the disconcerting knowledge that they were a 'lost army' – in the sense they were completely cut off from the world. At first they managed 11.5 miles (17 km) a day and then, as the country grew rougher, they 'settled down to the hard, stern graft of it'.

When it came to dealing with the Afghans to obtain supplies, Roberts insisted on strict discipline. There was no looting, even where locals exhibited hostility. Particular care was taken not to offend women, lest it infuriate the local men.

Everything was paid for in advance, including the 5,000 sheep purchased outside Kabul and corn bought from farmers along the route. Water and firewood were the most scarce resources, and so Roberts decided to purchase a few houses en route and had them stripped out for firewood. Water, however, while it could sometimes be located in villages or dug from seemingly dry beds, was often brackish.

The column was roused every morning at 0300, and set off an hour later. A conventional routine of ten minutes halt every hour was maintained throughout the day, with some longer rests in which meals were prepared. For the sake of security the marchers halted before 1900 hours each night, selecting positions they felt able to hold. The intense cold of the nights made sleep a rarity, while the dust raised by the march tormented every participant. It choked every throat, clogged everything and clung to the sweaty skin of each soldier. The camp followers proved to be the weak link in the whole expedition. Footsore or disheartened by the forced march, some began to lag behind despite the entreaties of the rest of the column. Crompton noted that even when threatened they would ask to be left to die. Others would deliberately slip away from the column at night and hide. Any deserters found by the Afghans were always murdered, as tribesmen believed that the skill of British surgeons meant wounded men would recover and return to take their revenge. They also believed that, if mutilated, these infidels would never enter paradise.

Roberts ensured that the Afghan garrison of Ghazni gave his force supplies, but soon after leaving the city, a number of observers noted that the Afghans had dug up a nearby cemetery where the fallen of the First Afghan War were buried. The Afghans had renamed the local settlement 'the resting place of martyrs' to commemorate their own dead, but had scattered the bones of British and Indian troops around on the surface. It was a stark and grisly reminder of the fate that would befall the column if they failed in this epic march.

At Kelat-i-Ghilzai (Qalat), Roberts collected the small British outpost force and learnt that Kandahar was still besieged. He also discovered that a sortie had been made, but that a number of casualties had been sustained. The garrison was nevertheless still intact and holding out. Roberts therefore ordered a day-long halt to allow his force to get some much-needed rest. The incidence of disease and heat injury had fortunately remained low and, despite everyone's fears, no cholera outbreaks had occurred. Roberts himself was ill after leaving Kelat, suffering a liver complaint, dyspepsia, headaches, chest pains and a loss of appetite. Feverish, he was unable to ride and had to be carried in a *dhoolie* (covered stretcher), but maintained his drive and made constant enquiries as to the welfare of the troops. This concern was reflected in the nicknames he earned from them: he was known affectionately as 'Bobs Bahadur' or 'Fighting Bobs'.

On 25 August, Roberts received more intelligence from Kandahar. It seemed that news of his approach had caused the Afghans to pull back from the immediate vicinity of Kandahar, and occupy a position around the Arghandab River. The move meant he had to be on guard in case the Afghan force decided to try and intercept him while he was strung out on the march, particularly as he possessed little artillery with which to fight a long-range action. The interception was not attempted, and his force soon reached Kandahar itself, where the anxious garrison cheered the relief column with enthusiasm. Roberts dragged himself back onto his horse to make the arrangements to re-establish a line of communication to India, and to start locating the enemy in order to make an immediate attack. Equipped with the garrison's 15 field guns, Roberts could take the offensive with confidence. His only grumbles were that those besieged in the citadel had exhibited little offensive spirit and had 'never even hoisted the Union Jack until the relieving force was close at hand'.

On 1 September, the day after the march had reached Kandahar, Roberts launched his men against the Afghan positions. Ayub Khan made a rapid escape and abandoned all of his artillery, and many of the tribesmen had already melted away to tend to their harvests. The remainder fought it out for as long as they could, losing more than 600 lives in the process. Highlanders and Gurkhas made a direct assault on the Afghan entrenchments with complete success. Roberts' losses were just 40 killed and 210 wounded.

What particularly pleased Roberts about the victory was the recovery of two British field guns lost at Maiwand, as well as a store of other guns and trophies. Yet he felt his crowning achievement was to have restored British military prestige after Maiwand. He believed this psychological achievement – for both the population of the region and at home – outweighed even the march from Kabul to Kandahar, which had been a true feat of endurance.

The political consequences of the war were rather mixed. Afghanistan returned to its status as a buffer state and the British found a suitably compliant ruler in the form of Amir Abdur Rahman. The Residency at Kabul was not rebuilt, and the British continued to rely on secret agents to keep abreast of intrigues in

Afghanistan during the Great Game, though no attempt was made by Russia to re-establish influence in the country until long after the British had quit India in the 1940s. The march from Kabul to Kandahar remained a celebrated event in Britain. The actions of Roberts had captured the essence of every relief march in aid of those beleaguered by assailants: the race against time, the endurance of the soldiers, the tough environment and the threats of sudden attack along the line of march by overwhelming numbers. Lord Roberts' force had come through all the challenges and fought a decisive battle right off the line of march. It was a brilliant success against the odds.

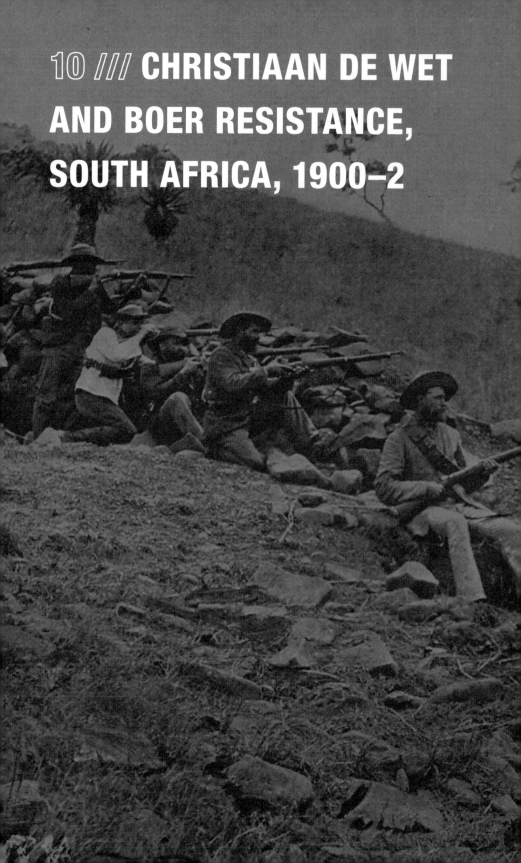

10 /// CHRISTIAAN DE WET AND BOER RESISTANCE, SOUTH AFRICA, 1900–2

An epic of endurance and determination, the *bittereinders* (bitter enders) of South Africa maintained a guerrilla campaign against vast numbers of British colonial forces and forced them to reach a generous peace at Vereeniging in 1902. The British high commissioner for Southern Africa, Sir Alfred Milner, and the secretary of state for the Colonies, Joe Chamberlain, had begun to grow anxious about the rapid increase in wealth and power of two Afrikaner republics that lay to the north. In 1886, the discovery of gold in the Transvaal acted as a magnet for foreign workers and led to the establishment of Johannesburg. Milner used the denial of civil and political rights to these workers as the pretext for diplomatic intervention. Exasperated by British pressure, the Transvaal Republic and the Orange Free State declared war on the British empire in October 1899. The Afrikaner generals led a swift invasion of colonial territory, hoping to inflict a sudden defeat that would force the British to make concessions. The British garrisons in Ladysmith, Kimberley and Mafeking, however, held out, denying the Boers their victory. British reinforcements arrived but initially made little headway in their retaliation, even suffering some serious setbacks. Soon even greater numbers were deployed, and by 1900 the British under Lord Roberts were steamrollering their way to the capitals of the two republics at Bloemfontein and Pretoria. Yet, while the conventional phase of the war was coming to an end in Britain's favour, many Boer fighters refused to accept defeat. They began to form small parties or 'commandos' of mounted men, often clustered around a skilful leader, and waged a guerrilla war against the occupation. While towns remained firmly in British hands, rural areas were not controlled. Attacks on colonial depots, outposts and railways increased dramatically towards the middle of the year 1900.

While some of the Transvaalers had despaired, the actions of General Christiaan de Wet and other rebels provided some encouragement. As early as 4 June, De Wet had led his mounted force to seize a much-needed convoy of supplies at Heilbron to the north of the Orange Free State and then, just two days later, he struck an inexperienced battalion of Derbyshire Militia guarding the bridge over the Rhenoster River. Attacking quickly, from various directions, De Wet used the element of surprise to cause confusion within the garrison. He exploited the disorder of the militia, compelling them to surrender, before using

Previous pages: **South African forces besieging Ladysmith, February 1900.**

their own ammunition to blow the bridge. Several columns were sent to intercept De Wet but they failed to locate him, finding only the trail of destruction he had left north of Kroonstad. The British reinforced the security of the railway lines with chains of defences and armoured trains, but the Orange Free State was beginning to stir, with more men joining the commandos. Roberts decided to send in three converging columns to press the commandos against the mountain ranges around the Brandwater Basin west of Ladysmith. At first the commandos gave ground and some considered using the mountains as a refuge, but others disagreed, believing they might become a trap, where, starved of supplies, the British would pick them off. De Wet argued that they should divide into four groups and break out of the British cordon to the west.

De Wet had persuaded his comrades in the nick of time. On 15 July 1900, under cover of darkness, his men slipped out of Slabbert's Pass while the British were bivouacking only a day's march away. Alerted to the move the next morning, the British cavalry and mounted infantry tried to pursue them, but were pinned down by De Wet's rearguard actions while the Afrikaners got their wagons of supplies safely away. Other Boers were not so lucky and found themselves cornered. Over 4,000 were forced to surrender and it seemed only a matter of time before De Wet and his confederates were tracked down in the same way. In fact, the British columns spent weeks pursuing De Wet, but he would ride, make feints, double back, change direction or fight seemingly at random. Meanwhile, in the western Transvaal, Koos de la Rey and Jan Smuts had ignited their own guerrilla war. Along with 7,000 men, they had based themselves south of the Magaliesberg Range, to the west of Pretoria, making raids across the region. Roberts strengthened the security of Pretoria with more troops and defences but was unable to suppress the guerrillas despite some spirited actions by his more isolated detachments.

De Wet crossed the central railway that ran northwards from the coast to Pretoria in early August, and eventually he reached the Vaal River. His objective was to enable the president of the Orange Free State, Martinus Steyn, to travel north to reach Paul Kruger, the President of the Transvaal, uniting the 'shadow' government. Afterwards De Wet planned to resume his guerrilla war, but the British had assembled 11,000 men to the south and intended to press him against one of three lines of defences – the Vaal River, the central railway or the Magaliesberg Range, where a further 18,000 British troops were operating.

Despite the sheer numbers operating against him, De Wet managed to keep one step ahead. He made use of the vast terrain to conceal his force, changing his route frequently. Taking care to look for unguarded gaps between British formations De Wet exploited the slow decision-making process of the larger British army and also strictly enforced a high level of discipline on his troops. A corps of European fighters led by Captain Danie Theron provided some experience in reconnaissance tasks too so that, by 14 August, De Wet had found his way through British lines, reached the Magaliesberg Range south of Pretoria and evaded all the attempts to cut him off. At Magaliesberg, De Wet's men scaled the mountains, crossing where – as locals described it – 'only monkeys dare roam'. His reputation for being a will-o'-the-wisp was growing, and it was providing inspiration to an Afrikaner population becoming increasingly bitter about British occupation.

To subjugate the resistance, General Horatio Herbert Kitchener reiterated proclamations against guerrilla activity and sent columns of infantry, cavalry and artillery out onto the veldt to track down and destroy the commandos. The mounted Boers could easily evade the slow-moving columns, and concentrated on picking off isolated parties and picquets. They would quickly ambush and, before the British could react, they would mount up and ride away. The columns could spend days searching fruitlessly, and they found it impossible to bring their greater firepower or numbers to bear. The Boers seemed to vanish and the British forces found themselves striking out at thin air.

The need to live off more meagre supplies and inflict as much damage as possible in more locations led De Wet to break up his commando into smaller fragments that could fight independently. The tactical merits of the guerrilla campaign were not in doubt, but from a strategic perspective it was difficult to see how the commandos could succeed. It is true that their effect was psychological as well as actual: they could keep the flame of resistance alive, but their chances of bringing the British to the negotiating table seemed very slim indeed. Moreover, by waging war in such a manner, the commandos risked losing the protection of the laws of war. When Lord Roberts handed over full command of the campaign to Kitchener, it seemed likely the British would take stricter measures against the Afrikaner population.

Realizing that the Boers were living off the support of sympathetic civilians in remote farmsteads, Kitchener decided to clear the veldt, herding as many civilians as possible into concentrated internment camps. Here they could be fed and housed, but also isolated from the commandos. The early experiments were not a success. In the camps many families lost women and children to epidemics of measles and mumps. Myths grew up that the British were deliberately trying to kill off Boer civilians, but it was really a matter of health, hygiene and inadequate organization. The clearances – which also involved the destruction of property, the confiscation or slaughter of livestock and the seizure of crops – not only caused an outcry in Britain but also persuaded the embittered commandos to fight on. Their cause, of resisting British occupation to the end, now seemed even more just. From a practical perspective, the re-housing of the civilians actually freed up the commandos: once the camps became better organized and the mortality rate subsided, many Boer fighters were confident that their families were protected.

The fighters were nevertheless confronted by the problem of logistics. While much of the veldt provided grazing for the horses, there was a shortage of rations for the commandos and ammunition for their German-made Mauser rifles. The Boers therefore took to following the British columns, gathering ammunition and tins of food that had been dropped by tired or overburdened troops. They also made daring raids to secure British Lee-Metford rifles and the food supplies they so desperately needed. By the end of the war, most Boers were armed with British weapons.

Unable to swat the commandos using lumbering columns, Kitchener devised a new strategy. He divided up the landscape into a series of gridded zones, each partitioned by barbed-wire fences and overlooked by hundreds of blockhouses. These fortified emplacements were garrisoned by a handful of troops equipped with communications equipment, food and ammunition, and they were positioned parallel to railway lines along which armoured trains steamed. The trains were mounted with searchlights and machine guns, and carried complements of reinforcements. As the fences snaked across the landscape, the commandos were pushed into smaller and smaller zones. Their freedom of movement was suddenly restricted and raiding became much more hazardous. To flush out the insurgents, Kitchener devised 'drives', with infantrymen spread in extended order over vast distances, marching steadily towards the fences and blockhouses. The aim was to crush the remaining insurgents in a great vice. The columns were scrapped; cavalry and mounted infantry units provided the British with more mobility.

In August 1900 De Wet had escaped at the Magaliesberg, but when he resumed attacks on the central railway he was repulsed at Frederikstadt and then hunted by a mounted British column led by Major-General Knox. When De Wet and Steyn met, settling down in a *laager* (defended camp) while laying plans to take the war into the British-held Cape Colony, they were surprised by part of Knox's column in a dawn attack. Colonel Le Gallais, the British commander, was wounded in the assault but his men continued the attack. Initially De Wet fled but he returned to assist the troops left behind in a four-hour gun battle. As De Wet tried to get into action, more British mounted infantry arrived, and he was driven off. All De Wet's weapons and wagons were lost, and 100 of his men were taken prisoner, wounded or killed.

Despite this, De Wet was undeterred. He quickly recruited 1,500 men and headed for Dewetsdorp, a settlement named after his father. There he made a raid and took with him British prisoners, who had to endure severe privations and brutal punishment. Believing De Wet was heading for the Orange River, Knox was again in pursuit. De Wet just managed to keep ahead, hiding in the broken country and moving at night to evade mounted patrols. He drove his men hard, denying them any form of baggage except rifles and ammunition. Although he was ostensibly conducting a guerrilla campaign, he was, in effect, really a fugitive on the run. It was at this point, however, that the commandos still in the field decided to play a strategic ace. They would send a number of groups into the Cape Colony to persuade the Afrikaner population there to rebel against the British. De Wet would take 2,200 men into the Cape itself and ride for Cape Town once the rebellion was underway. Just as Kitchener was being forced to combat a series diversionary raids in the east, he learnt through his intelligence service of the projected 'invasion' of the Cape. On 27 January 1901, Kitchener formed 12 columns and rushed troops along the railways that followed the Orange River. The De Wet hunt was underway in earnest.

De Wet used scouts far ahead of his main force to ascertain where the British were strongest, and from this discovered the newly reinforced line. Employing all his skills of deception and fieldcraft, he took the bulk of his men across the Orange River near Colesburg, though the remainder refused to leave their homeland on what they saw as a fool's errand. Only 15 hour's ride behind De Wet, the British were soon alert to the crossing. More men took up the chase, including a force of Australians and New Zealanders eager to prove their worth. The pursuers forced De Wet to turn north but heavy rain hampered all movement, with veldt trails turning to muddy morasses, but De Wet drove his men even harder and eventually returned to his westward course. Yet attempts to join up with other commandos failed because of the British columns now swarming into the threatened area. Kitchener deployed 15 more formations along 160 miles (260 km) of the Cape railway. Each one was ordered to sweep westwards and, if it lost contact with the Boers, to return to the railway line to be redeployed further south. This gave the British formation a series of prongs that threatened to cut off De Wet, while the rest of the columns marched southwards.

With his men exhausted by the endless forced marches through the night, the atrocious weather and the cloying mud, De Wet realized the danger he was now in. He had no alternative but to turn back. The problem was that he now had to track eastwards along the southern bank of the Orange River, caught in a quadrangle formed by three increasingly reinforced railway lines and the raging river. Each drift, or ford, had been rendered impassable by floodwaters. On 24 February, he at last found a drift that was relatively unguarded and that the horses could swim. The Boers were pursued for another two weeks but just managed to stay ahead until the British lost the scent in mid-March.

Afrikaner guerrilla resistance developed across Transvaal and Orange River Colony after British victories. Commandos evaded British forces to strike at railways and settlements so successfully that major hunts were made for their leaders, including Christiaan de Wet.

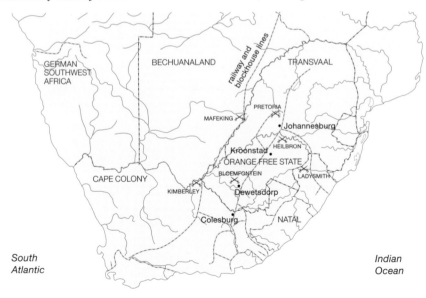

De Wet had managed to traverse 800 miles (1,300 km) of territory and tie up 15,000 British and imperial troops, but had failed to ignite the expected Cape Dutch rebellion. His men, moreover, were worn out by the experience and vowed never to attempt to resurrect the plan. De Wet went to ground, dispersing his men to avoid capture, while other commandos did their best to continue to attack isolated detachments and hinder British forces. Their only hope now lay in staying in the field long enough to convince the British the campaign was no longer worth the cost.

In fact Kitchener continued to improve his defensive railway lines and extend wire fences and blockhouses across the countryside. Each area was still being subdivided into smaller areas to limit the remaining commandos' freedom of movement. Blockhouses appeared in prefabricated form and were quickly assembled, sometimes at intervals of only 200 yards (180 m). Eventually there would be 3,700 miles (6,000 km) of fencing and 8,000 blockhouses, guarded by 50,000 troops and 16,000 African levies. The British also kept up their night raids and continued to scour the country with columns. In July 1901 the entire Free State 'shadow' government was captured, and in August Jan Smuts' attempt to make another incursion into the Cape (while managing to stay intact and ahead of the British) nevertheless failed to elicit strong support. By October, there were 64 British columns operating against the remaining commandos, and each column had a mounted element that could set off in pursuit, freeing itself from the slower-moving supply wagons and their infantry escorts.

The commandos had pledged to fight to the 'bitter end', but the bitter end had now come. Supplies dwindled. Many of their horses died, forcing the Boers to make exhausting treks to stay one step ahead of their pursuers. Hundreds of fighters were captured and made prisoners of war. Thousands of *hensoppers* ('hands-uppers'; those abandoning the struggle) surrendered, and many of these disillusioned men then became 'joiners' and actually enlisted as auxiliary forces in the British army. By 1902, the majority of Afrikaners were eager to see the war, which had lasted four years, brought to an end. The British government started to talk of a 'magnanimous gesture' in their offers of peace and it seemed to be only a matter of time before the remaining commandos were caught, killed or died of starvation.

De Wet had waited until February 1902, when the South African spring had returned, before calling on his men to step up operations, and he made a particular point of avoiding areas close to the new lines of blockhouses or the railways.

Roaming deep across the veldt, he was able to surprise the 11th Imperial Yeomanry at Tweefontein. However, the tide was clearly turning: 700 Boer fighters were captured by the new all-mounted columns in night raids (the commandos often moved at night) or in dawn raids, when laagers of tired commandos were easily surprised. Kitchener deployed 9,000 men to sweep up De Wet in a thoroughly systematic cordon operation whereby a line of mounted men would patrol across the veldt, searching every location, before the entire line set off again. At night, the lines would dig entrenchments and wait for the Boers to try and make a breakout. Twice De Wet did precisely that, the second time using a charge of 1,000 fighters and a stampede of cattle to pierce the British line. Yet De Wet had lost 1,200 men in the encounters. Many more were now without horses, trudging on foot mile after mile, anxiously glancing behind them for signs of mounted British pursuers. De la Rey assisted the hard-pressed De Wet by stepping up attacks further west, and making spectacular assaults on well-armed columns, but the erosion of commando numbers was obvious. When the British offered negotiations, it was clear that the opportunity had to be taken.

De Wet and Steyn represented the most diehard opinion among the Afrikaners, with De Wet consistently opposed to any talk of giving up the independence of the two Boer republics. Others, including Smuts, argued that it was no longer a case of fighting to the bitter end, for the bitter end had come. Steyn resigned and De Wet became the acting president of the Orange Free State. Bolstered by the views of his remaining fighters, he maintained his implacable opposition to any compromise with the British, until his was the only voice left not in favour of peace. Finally, a personal appeal from Louis Botha and De la Rey changed his mind, and he accepted the British peace offer, thus ending the war.

Embodying the determination of the Afrikaners to sustain their independence and to resist to the end, De Wet had exhibited perhaps the greatest persistence of all the famous commando leaders. Critics argued that he was really famous only because of his escapes, rather than his ability to change the course of the war, however his real achievement was to keep the flame of resistance alive despite overwhelming odds. That he did so with skill, ruthlessness and devotion to a cause only increases that prowess still further.

11 /// THE DEVONS AT BOIS DES BUTTES, FRANCE, 1918

T he 2nd Battalion, the Devonshire Regiment was entirely wiped out in this last stand during the First World War when attacked by overwhelming numbers of German troops. The Devons' sacrifice bought time for other units to regroup and offer resistance along the River Aisne at a crucial moment in the campaign. For their selfless actions that day, this entire regiment of stoic West Country men was awarded the Croix de Guerre, the highest decoration France could bestow on an ally.

In early 1918 the mood among the Allies was, at best, one of grim determination. Germany had knocked Russia out of the war the previous spring. It had inflicted such heavy casualties on the French in Champagne that mutinies had broken out on the Chemin des Dames. Italy had been dealt a body blow at Caporetto by a combined Austro-German force. The Allies could at least celebrate the fall of Baghdad, taken from Turkish control, and they could look forward to the influx of American troops now that the United States had joined the war, but there was little optimism. Everyone knew that Germany would bring fresh divisions from Russia across to the Western Front, and that they would swarm over the Allied defences. Britain had already lost so many men that some units had to be dismantled and new composite formations created. Divisions were reduced from four brigades to three. There were many conscripted men with little heart for the war, and when the German offensive finally began, the barrage of gunfire (*Trommelfeuer*) tore apart the Allied front lines. Many troops, finding German storm troops infiltrating their positions, simply packed it in and surrendered. Staff officers, riding forward to gauge the situation, found dejected soldiers streaming towards the rear, some unarmed, having cast away their weapons.

But not every regiment behaved this way. The 2nd Battalion, the Devonshire Regiment, led by Lieutenant-Colonel R. H. Anderson-Morshead, fought it out to the last man. These proud British soldiers clung to their smashed and pulverized trenches, and stubbornly battled on to buy time for units further back. Certain of their own destruction, 29 officers and 552 other ranks refused to let the Germans pass and went down fighting. The last man to see them alive described the Commanding Officer, surrounded by a handful of soldiers, still calmly giving orders. He told his surviving troops: 'Your job for England, men, is to hold the

Previous pages: **Painting of the last stand of the 2nd Devons at Bois des Buttes, 27 May 1918.**

blighters up as much as you can, to give our troops a chance on the other side of the river [Aisne]. There is no hope of relief. We have to fight to the last.' Fetching his pipe from his pocket as the Germans showered his trench with stick grenades, mortars and machine-gun fire, the colonel listened to his orderly's warning that the Boche were closing in. He told the young soldier, without any emotion: 'Well, Jordan, we shall have to make the best of it.' This was the sort of quiet courage that had made the British army famous in countless other battles, but it was surely displayed to an extraordinary degree at Bois des Buttes.

Having already completed a gruelling period in the trenches around Ypres, the Devons had been reallocated to a so-called 'quiet sector' at Bois des Buttes on the River Aisne in late May 1918. The German offensive had begun in March, and it still retained its potency. As a mixture of more experienced men and the new battle casualty replacements marched up to the front line, they were aware of the general situation. There was the usual grumbling, but something of the regiment's traditions and pride kept the troops at their posts. No one was going to let their comrades down, or besmirch their reputation.

The position the Devons were ordered to occupy consisted of two small and sandy hills surrounded by woodland. The badly constructed trenches in front had almost no field of fire, and could be approached through the foliage. Worse, all the positions were well known to German gunners. As the British troops tried to gain some sense of the ground in the dark, their artillery kept up a steady bombardment of the German lines. The Germans, for their part, sent over an occasional gas shell, forcing the Devons into stifling masks.

On 27 May, Anderson-Morshead just had time to call together his company commanders and inform them that a major German attack was to be expected at 0100 hours before, with Teutonic precision, the firestorm was unleashed at exactly that moment. A hurricane of HE (high-explosive rounds) caused trench walls to cave in and the soldiers had to shelter as best they could in dugouts, masks on to ward off the poison gas. The defences in front of the Devons were completely obliterated. Trees were smashed into matchwood. Heavy boughs were hurled across the battlefield, wire cut through by white-hot shards of shells. The bombardment exacted a heavy toll; no one outside a trench or dugout survived, and it soon became evident to the Commanding Officer that his communications had been completely severed.

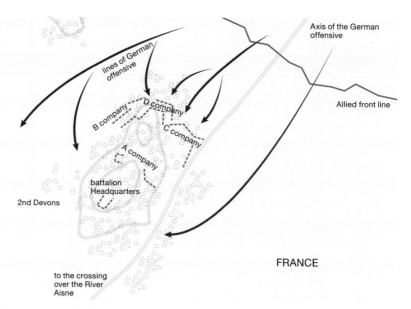

At Bois des Buttes, a single British battalion fought to the death rather than give up their position, despite overwhelming German numbers. Their devotion to duty, and to the defence of France, earned them the highest French military honour: the Croix de Guerre.

As the first streaks of dawn appeared, Anderson-Morshead knew he could not risk his men being caught sheltering underground. Lieutenant Clarke, commanding B Company, ordered his men to fan out into the ruins of the trenches facing northwest. To their right, in the centre of the line and facing north, was D Company under Lieutenant Harris, and a little further out, facing north and east, was C Company under Lieutenant Tindal. A Company and Battalion Headquarters held the highest knoll in reserve. German shelling had barely abated, and wounded men could not reach the aid posts to the rear of the knoll. Lieutenant Kane, an American medical officer, did what he could in a hopeless situation. Worse, the heavy shelling also meant that runners could not get forward to the companies, effectively blinding the battalion. Messengers to brigade headquarters never arrived, and a combination of heavy mist, dust and smoke obscured the front. Then news started to trickle in. The Germans had simply marched over the Allied front lines to the north and were already making their way past the Devons to the east. Small parties of survivors trying to escape from the front were being cut down by the thousands of German troops in pursuit. Grenades, often clustered together, were thrown into every dugout the Germans encountered during their advance. The Allied defence was collapsing.

As the German gunners lifted their sights to bombard the area behind the Devons, the companies got their first sight of the advancing masses. They could see them streaming forward, their transport and guns coming on behind. Above, German aircraft made ground-strafing runs. It was clear that any attempt to withdraw would mean death in the gunfire, but it was also evident that the handful of Devons could not hope to survive against the numbers now approaching. B Company was the first to engage, using its two Lewis machine guns to mow down the lines now coming on. The Germans closed up, paused to launch a cascade of rifle grenades and again dashed forward. Corporal Leat of B Company described how he and his comrades had 'blazed away' until the first attack had been cut down. A second wave met the same grisly fate, but the third wave was simply overwhelming: the Germans closed in using stick grenades and rifle fire at close quarters. Isolated groups of Devons were wiped out, but the few who remained kept up their defiant resistance. Individuals dropped back, returning fire until the last safe moment, then dashed back again – some moving further in towards their battalion headquarters.

In fact men from Headquarters Company had started to get forward to bolster the line. Lieutenant Maunder grabbed any men he could from the old front line units and formed a ragged defence. It was becoming evident that B Company had practically ceased to exist, and a good deal of fire was now pouring in from the west. But to the east the situation was also critical. Lieutenant Tindal, the commander of C Company, was told by the survivors of the old front line that the Germans were going to envelop his right. The defences they had, such as they were, would offer no protection against this, but Tindal believed that a counter-attack might knock the Germans off balance and stem their advance. The company's single Lewis gun suppressed the enemy for a while, but all too soon it was knocked out and the Germans were once more coming on in such numbers that Tindal feared his little force would soon be overrun. More than half his command had been killed or wounded. In this moment of desperation, he ordered his men to fix bayonets and charge: they did so, scrambling over the parapet into a hail of fire. Within a few yards they were stopped, caught in a barbed-wire entanglement and sprayed with fire from an entire German battalion. Those who survived went to ground.

Within minutes fire was coming in on C Company from several directions. Wounded Devons kept up what fire they could from shell holes, and some, such as Private Greenslade, personally hunted down German machine gunners by crawling from place to place, and shooting from any available cover. Tindal was killed sniping against a German officer. Private Knight and five others, finding themselves completely surrounded in an old trench, fought back to back. A party of five men on the road that ran to the east of the knoll engaged in a close-quarter battle out in the open, and were all cut down. D Company was also being overwhelmed. One trench was disputed by both sides but the Devons, although outnumbered, fought their way into the opponent's half in textbook fashion, lobbing a grenade and dashing forward after the blast to shoot or bayonet whoever was left alive. Twice they lost, and twice they recaptured this position, until shells and bombs destroyed what was left of the fortification. Survivors of the battle spoke highly of the young British officers who did their best to cheer their men on, find them good firing positions and set an example of physical courage.

At this point the Germans were inside the Devons' position and fighting their way up to the battalion's headquarters. The remnants of D Company refused to give in and kept up their fire from shell holes and broken trenches. C and B Company were almost wiped out. Anderson-Morshead gathered together what remained of his force and positioned them to the rear of the main knoll, although this provided scant shelter against the machine-gun fire that rained down from three directions. A second move was therefore made – and three parties were formed to create a final defensive ring on the road at the base of the hill.

By now the Germans had closed to within a few yards of the survivors, and the final hours were a desperate battle between the dwindling band of Devons and the determined, experienced and more numerous soldiers of the Kaiser. The German troops believed this was the final offensive of the war and so were motivated to finish off the resistance of the Western Allies. But to secure victory they needed to push on quickly, bypassing any strongpoints to reach the rear areas of the British and French forces. The Devons were holding things up. Vital time was being lost by the Germans. Indeed, the attacks at the end of May were to be the last push of the German army on the Western Front, as the impetus of their offensive petered out. By July, the Germans were on the back foot.

At Bois des Buttes in May 1918, however, the Germans were still confident of victory. Anderson-Morshead knew that there was no way out for the 2nd Battalion. The last man to leave them, an officer of the Royal Artillery, noted the coolness of the men that remained behind, and of the colonel in particular: he was 'calmly writing his notes with a perfect hail of HE round him'. The Regimental Sergeant Major, and the Adjutant Captain Burke – the only other leaders left alive – also gave their words of encouragement to the last few soldiers.

Then, finally, the last men were cut down; grenades and bullets finished them off and the Germans surged on past the hill. But the Devons had achieved their mission: the Germans had been held up for a precious few hours that allowed the Allies time to organize the defences to the rear. It must also have sounded a dread warning to the German army: against all the odds, and contrary to the hopeless nature of their position, the British had proved that they were not yet willing to be beaten. The Kaiser's army had expected everything to give way before their over-whelming mass, but the defiant resistance of the Allied units on the Western Front – units such as the Devons – must have caused doubts to creep into the minds of the German High Command. Indeed, the spring of 1918 marked the high point of the German tide on the Western Front. Within six months the German army was bundled back towards their own frontier and in November they were compelled to sue for peace. The Devons' sacrifice, small as it was in the context of a brutal war, had not been in vain.

T he Battle of Warsaw marked a turning point in the course of the Polish–
Soviet War (February 1919–March 1921), and it is often attributed with
having defeated a communist offensive that otherwise would have rolled
across Europe. The Spartacists (a German communist group led by Rosa
Luxemburg and Karl Liebknecht) had already established a correspondence with
Vladimir Lenin's Bolsheviks in Moscow and were planning to synchronize a *coup
d'état* with the arrival of Red Army troops. There were communist revolts breaking
out in Berlin, Munich and Budapest. Red revolutionary flags had been hoisted by
disaffected German soldiers, angry at the outcome of the First World War. In
Britain, the decision to assist anti-communist forces with an armed intervention
in Russia led to protests among some British workers. When the government in
London offered to send military supplies to Poland, the Trades Union Congress
threatened a general strike. French socialists were just as militant. The left-wing
newspaper *L'Humanité* announced: 'Not a Man, not a sou, not a shell for reactionary
and capitalist Poland. Long Live the Russian Revolution! Long Live the Workmen's
International!'

In Russia, Lenin and the Bolsheviks had argued for some time that commu-
nism could not survive if it was confined to one country. Leon Trotsky, commanding
the Red Army, spoke of the need for a world revolution. Lenin believed the more
advanced industrialized economies of Western Europe were ripe for revolution, and
that the Reds had only to march through Poland to link up with the revolutionaries
there. Nikolai Bukharin, a leading writer for the communist newspaper *Pravda*,
declared that the Red Army should push on 'right up to London and Paris'. The
vast size of the Russian population had always created concern in central Europe
about the military potential of their eastern neighbour, and, despite the defeat of
the Russian armies in the First World War, the prospect of hundreds of thousands
of ideologically enthused communists linking up with the Russian armed forces
(regarded as a 'steamroller') was alarming to the European elites. European workers
appeared to be seething with discontent and ready to revolt.

To make matters worse, the Poles and Ukrainians – who had enjoyed some
initial successes against the Russians in early 1919 – were in full retreat by the following summer. Some 800,000 Red Army troops had overcome the bulk of their

Previous pages: **General Piłsudski reviews his troops, Warsaw, 1920.**

'White' anti-communist enemies within Russia, contained the foreign intervention-
ist forces from the West and were pursuing the Poles across the Steppes towards
Warsaw. They were moving at a remarkable speed, covering about 20 miles (32 km)
a day, which gave the Poles barely any chance to regroup. The first Polish defensive
line, in the Ukraine on the Auta River, was pierced in four days of bitter fighting at
the beginning of July 1920. The second attempt to stem the Russians took place
along a line of old German trenches in mid-July, but there were simply too few
Polish troops to hold every part of the line in strength. Spread across a front of
200 miles (320 km), the Russian forces infiltrated, bypassed and continued to press
the Poles back at every point. General Semyon Budyonny's 1st Cavalry Army swept
deep into the Polish rear and captured the Warsaw neighbourhood of Bródno. For
a time it appeared the Polish forces would be enveloped and swallowed up. A Polish
attempt to regroup on the River Bug was initially successful and the Russians were
held for a week, but, while the Poles planned a counter-offensive, the fortress of
Brest-Litovsk – the concentration point of their attack – fell to the Soviet 16th
Army as soon as it was assaulted. The Polish army was in disarray. Soldiers in rags
and bare feet were in full retreat. Defeat seemed imminent.

General Tukhachevsky, who commanded the Soviet armies of the Northwest
Front, exclaimed to his troops: 'To the West! Over the corpse of White Poland lies
the road to worldwide conflagration. ... Onward to Berlin over the corpse of
Poland!' Similarly enthusiastic reports were being issued in Moscow. Indeed, so
self-evident did the victory seem that Josef Stalin, the chief Political Commissar for
the neighbouring Southwest Front, took a portion of the Red Army to seize Lvov
in the hope of gaining greater recognition. The rest of the Southwest Front armies
marched towards the region of Galicia as planned, but Budyonny's cavalry also
disobeyed instructions and sought to have the glory of entering Lvov first. This
decision was to prove costly to the Soviets. Instead of covering the southern
approaches to Warsaw as planned, Budyonny and Stalin had left a gap that the
Polish army could exploit. Of equal magnitude was the breaking of Soviet ciphers,
which gave the Poles access to Soviet signals traffic. Not only did this allow the
Poles to read diplomatic messages, but it also helped them determine where and
when Soviet formations would move, as well as their strengths and their armaments. It was through these decrypted intercepts that the Poles learnt of the gap
that had appeared in the Russian advance.

General Józef Piłsudski, commander of the Polish forces, was well aware of the critical nature of the military situation, but he conceived a bold plan to save Warsaw. The scheme was so daring that even some of his subordinates did not believe it could work. It seemed a desperate last gamble. First, the Polish army had to be reinforced rapidly. Fortunately, as the army fell back, its lines of communication shortened, making the passage of information and supplies easier. Fresh forces could be called up. Once a defensive line had been stabilized, the Polish forces were deliberately to fall back in good order across the Vistula River to draw the Soviets on towards Warsaw. Of all the troops available, Piłsudski intended to keep a quarter to the south ready for a strategic counter-offensive that would cut across the axis of the Russian advance. To the northwest of the capital, the Polish 5th Army would hold back until the Russians were fully committed to their attack, then they too would be unleashed, cutting into the rear of the Soviet lines of communication.

Piłsudski concentrated a corps of 20,000 men as the main fist of his southern counter-offensive. He selected the best of his units for this critical task, and reinforced each of the wings with elements of the Polish 3rd Army and 4th Army. Positioned along the Wieprz River, they were poised to strike. They were still gravely outnumbered, however. If the Soviets detected them, and they were engaged, the entire plan would fail. A number of officers feared that this would happen as the Russians advanced on a broad front. Some even condemned the plan as 'amateurish'. Moreover, such was the haste in which the plan was conceived that logistical arrangements had not been completed by the time the battle began. Units were attempting to reorganize within a days' march of the advancing Russians, and many were still under strength. Often units were also equipped with weapons from a variety of countries, creating confusion in ammunition resupply.

Fortunately for Piłsudski, the Soviets on the southern side of the advance had lost contact with the Polish forces in front of them, and they did not detect the build-up. Tukhachevsky's plan was simply to advance towards Warsaw, seize river crossings north and south of the city, and then launch the main offensive from the northwest, curling around the city to the north and cutting off the Polish supply routes from the coast. The southern flank was to be held by the Mazyr (or Mozyrska) Group, a single infantry division of 8,000 men whose role was really only to maintain a link between the Northwest Front and the Southwest Front.

//

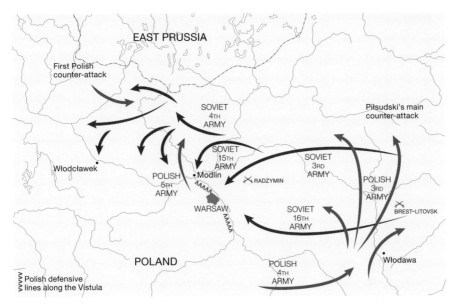

EAST PRUSSIA

First Polish
counter-attack

SOVIET
4TH
ARMY

Piłsudski's main
counter-attack

SOVIET
15TH
ARMY

SOVIET
3RD
ARMY

Włodcławek

POLISH
5TH
ARMY

• Modlin

RADZYMIN

POLISH
3RD
ARMY

BREST-LITOVSK

WARSAW

SOVIET
16TH
ARMY

POLAND

POLISH
4TH
ARMY

Włodawa

Polish defensive
lines along the Vistula

The Bolshevik Red Army seemed to be unstoppable as it advanced westwards, but General Piłsudski conceived a bold plan to use smaller, more agile divisions against the vast and less manoeuvrable Russian forces.

The initial and rapid successes of the Red Army as it strode forward, however, unnerved Piłsudski. Four Russian armies were moving on to the capital, and the fall of Radzymin, a fortified town just a few miles from the city's outskirts, forced Piłsudski to bring his entire plan forward by 24 hours. On 12 August, Polish and Russian forces each attempted to take control of the area around Radzymin. Fighting continued all day and night, and the Poles waited until dawn on 13 August to evacuate the fortress of Modlin. The pressure of Soviet numbers was overwhelming. Everywhere the Poles were being forced back.

At this critical juncture, the 203rd Uhlan Cavalry Regiment made a courageous and seemingly suicidal charge. Breaking through the Russian lines they continued into depth and overran the radio command post of the Soviet 4th Army. Realizing that the Soviets in this sector had only one other frequency open, the Polish army sent continuous jamming signals. Deprived of communications, the Russian formation was thrown into chaos.

The Soviets, meanwhile, had reached the capital, and were contesting the suburbs with the Polish 1st and 5th Armies. General Józef Haller, with overall command of Polish forces in the northern sector, realized the gravity of the situation. He knew that Piłsudski's southern counter-offensive was not ready to be launched, and so he took the initiative – advancing to engage the Soviet divisions that were now crowding into the plains north of the city and heading in his direction. Although outnumbered and outgunned, the 5th Army held the Soviets at Nasielsk between 14 and 15 August. The recapture of Radzymin at the same time lifted Polish morale at a critical moment. With the Russians forces halted, the 5th Army went over to the counter-attack and used all the tanks and armoured cars the Polish army could muster to drive deep into the areas behind the Soviets.

On 16 August, aware that the tipping point had come, Piłsudski unleashed his southern counter-offensive. The Soviet Mazyr Group was crushed by one Polish division and a cavalry brigade, while the other four divisions under Piłsudski's personal command met no opposition at all. They pushed forward 28 miles (45 km) on the first day, severing Soviet communications and supply routes. On the first night the town of Włodawa was also recovered. By the middle of the second day, the Polish counter-offensive was continuing northwards, slicing its way through the supply system of the Soviet forces and embedding itself 45 miles (70 km) in the rear of the Russian armies. Tukhachevsky realized what was happening and issued orders for the Russian forces to halt and change axis in an attempt to shorten his front, recover his lines of communication and counter-attack. But it was too late. Some units did not get the orders, while others tried to press on towards Warsaw. Some just halted. The result was total confusion. The only Soviet formation to retain cohesion was the 15th Army, which managed not only to extract itself but also to shield the collapsing Northwest Front.

In the north, the Polish 5th Army continued to make progress on its own account. The Polish 1st Infantry Division made a remarkable forced march to cover over 160 miles (260 km) in just six days, placing itself deep in the Soviet rear. The result was that reinforcements for the Soviet 16th Army were intercepted and checked. Deprived of supplies, orders and ammunition, many Russian troops decided to surrender.

Three Russian armies had fallen apart, and their troops were either surrendering or streaming to the east in a desperate bid to escape the pursuing Polish forces. The Russian 3rd Cavalry Corps continued advancing and managed to cross the border into Germany. There it was halted and, given that hostilities had not

//

been declared against Germany, it was interned. Some 15,000 Russian soldiers had been killed in Piłsudski's manoeuvre, with a further 10,000 wounded and 65,000 taken prisoner. Polish losses were 4,500 killed and 22,000 wounded. The Poles also captured over 230 artillery pieces and more than 1,000 machine guns. But the most important result was the failure of the Bolshevik offensive. While supremely confident of victory in early August, the Russians had been driven back on every line by the middle of the month. After the battle, Tukhachevsky tried to rally and reorganize his armies. He formed a defensive line along the Niemen River, but was broken again in a six-day engagement in September. With the Bolshevik forces hurrying rearwards, Moscow readily accepted the ceasefire brokered by France and Britain.

Piłsudski had achieved something that most had considered impossible. Heavily outnumbered and with his own forces retreating, he had executed a brilliantly bold, if extremely risky, counter-offensive. The appearance of his divisions from an unexpected direction, and the severing of the Soviet lines of communication, caused utter confusion in the Russian headquarters. The loss of cohesion and momentum, combined with the continuing pressure of the Polish forces, initiated the sudden collapse of the Bolshevik armies, and the Polish counter-offensive at Warsaw gave rise to the belief that Poland had effectively saved Europe from a Bolshevik invasion. The Soviets did indeed abandon hopes for a march westwards into Europe and concentrated instead on the consolidation of power within most of the territories of the former Russian empire. Their expansionism was contained thanks to the daring plan of General Piłsudski, and, as it came to be known, 'the miracle on the Vistula'.

13 /// THE WINTER WAR, FINLAND, 1939–40

On 30 November 1939, Soviet troops with a numerical advantage of more than five to one poured across the remote and wintry border of Finland. The ominous low hum of Soviet aircraft, wave after wave, was matched on the ground by the roaring and clanking of hundreds of advancing tanks. Waiting deep in the forest were Finnish troops and mobilized citizen soldiers, dressed in white winter camouflage but equipped with precious few anti-tank weapons. Their forward scouts watched the Soviets lumbering up the handful of roads, then flitted away on skis. Coordinating their movements, the outnumbered Finnish ski troops took up positions on either side of the Soviet columns, and initiated a series of ambushes with mines and small-arms fire. The Soviets were thrown into confusion, and their regiments blundered in different directions only to be ambushed afresh. As darkness fell, individual Soviet units tried to form defensive positions, and were raided, harried and attacked again and again. The Finns called these isolated enemy formations *mottis*, and while some Soviet garrisons fought bravely, others collapsed or were overrun. The mighty Soviet offensive was in trouble from the outset, and although the attackers could bring to bear massive resources, the Finns were to prove a formidable adversary against these incredible odds.

The Soviet Union had inherited much of the old Russian empire but it had not regained possession of Finland. This independent country had been conquered by the tsar in 1809, but wrested back some autonomy in 1905. In 1917, during the Russian Revolution, Finland reasserted its independence, throwing Bolshevik forces out of the country. In 1921, the Finns assisted anti-Bolshevik rebels across the border, and in retaliation the Russians orchestrated a raid called the Pork Mutiny in 1922. Unable to crush the Finns militarily, the Bolsheviks had concentrated on trying to subvert the Finnish constitution by backing communist activists. The Finnish communist party proved unpopular, however, and by the 1930s the threat of political violence or a coup appeared to have been contained. A non-aggression pact, concluded by Stalin, marked the end of the period of rivalry in foreign relations, although the Soviet government continued to press for territorial concessions that would give greater security to Leningrad, positioned as it was so close to the border with Finland.

Previous pages: **A fast-moving section of Finnish 'ghost troops' on skis.**

The most significant change in Soviet policy came in August 1939 when a deal was struck with Adolf Hitler's Germany. While ostensibly a settlement of differences and a mutual promise not to wage war on the other, secret clauses allowed Germany the freedom to crush Poland, and gave Stalin a free hand further east. The Nazis invaded Poland in September, and Soviet forces annexed the remaining territory in November. The Baltic states were threatened and ordered to permit the construction of Soviet military or naval bases on their soil. But Finland, sensing it was next, began a secret and gradual mobilization. As expected, the Soviets increased the pressure on Finland for territorial concessions, deploying more troops along the border throughout October and November 1939. On 26 November, the Soviet border post at Mainila was inexplicably shelled, and the Soviet government was quick to condemn Finland as the aggressor. In fact, the attack may have been carried out by Soviet secret police to provide the necessary *casus belli* for an invasion.

Four days after the bombardment of Mainila, 21 Soviet divisions – totalling 450,000 men – rolled across the Finnish border, and the capital, Helsinki, was subjected to an intense air raid. The Soviets were organized into four armies. Starting on the southern border, the Seventh Army was positioned to strike north against the city of Viipuri and to destroy Finnish forces on the Karelian Isthmus. The start line of Eighth Army was north of Lake Ladoga, and its mission was to advance northwards and then to cut in behind the Finnish defences. The Ninth Army was deployed on the eastern border of Finland, and its purpose was to drive deep into Finland and cut the country in two. The Fourteenth Army was positioned in the far north, and its objective was the port of Petsamo in northern Finland. These armies were supported by an air armada of nearly 4,000 bombers and fighter planes. There was confidence in the Soviet high command that the campaign would be concluded swiftly. Poland had fallen in three weeks, and they believed that Finland would be overrun and defeated in a fortnight.

But Finland was not Poland. The open landscape of eastern Poland was perfect tank country, whereas Finland was covered in dense forests and lakes. There were few roads and large areas were marshy, although in winter the frozen ground presented less of a problem. Perhaps more importantly, the Polish army had been largely defeated by the Nazis before the Soviets had attacked, and so the easy victory had not tested the Soviet military. When confronted by more significant resistance, the inefficiencies of the Soviet armed forces would be exposed. Stalin had purged the officer corps of most of its brightest and most talented members, favouring loyalty and obedience above all else. As a result, more than 36,000 officers had been imprisoned, worked to exhaustion in labour camps or executed, and the remainder dared not exercise too much initiative for fear of arousing the suspicions of the omnipresent political commissars. These agents of Stalin were likely to denounce anyone who did not use the correct rhetoric or toe the party line, and a denunciation could be deadly. The effect on the battlefield was to curb risk-taking and manoeuvring, giving the Finns the opportunity to hit and run, or to isolate and destroy static formations.

The Finns knew it would be impossible to guard the entire 600-mile (1,000-km) frontier, and so they opted for a system of defence in depth. By drawing the Soviets into the forested interior, they could force them to push along a small number of tracks and avenues. Such predictable routes made it possible to make their attacks, using surprise and precision to nullify the Soviet advantage in numbers. The most vulnerable part of the Finnish border was the Karelian Isthmus, where the landscape was more rolling. Six divisions were deployed there, and a defensive belt, the Mannerheim Line, was constructed. While Soviet propagandists later tried to exaggerate the strength of this line, the fact was that it consisted of little more than a ribbon of trenches and some bunkers revetted with logs. Every effort had been made to take advantage of the terrain, with fields of fire that enfiladed the Soviets' likely lines of approach. The chief problem was a lack of manpower. Regular Finnish forces were concentrated in the most vulnerable southern and eastern sectors (three corps and one corps respectively), and this left the north in the hands of border guards, militia and some reservists.

As the Soviets advanced towards the Mannerheim Line on 30 November 1939, Finnish ski troops fought delaying actions. Courageously, they got as close to the Soviet tanks as possible and thrust logs or iron bars into the tracks and running gear to immobilize them. A few tanks would then block the entire Soviet column. Petrol bombs – the famous Molotov cocktail, named after the Soviet Foreign Minister who coveted their country – were also hurled onto the rear decks of Soviet tanks or dropped into the open hatches of vehicles that had been halted. When the Soviets tried to employ the full weight of their supporting fire, the Finns would melt away. It was a successful tactic. North of Lake Ladoga, at Tolvajärvi, the Soviet 139th Motor Rifle Division was defeated by a much smaller force of Finnish troops.

Soon, however, things were to swing back in the Soviets' favour, and by 4 December, a crisis was occurring north of Lake Ladoga. The Soviets had hammered the Finnish defences with devastating volumes of artillery fire and troops there had begun to fall back. The retreat was in danger of becoming a rout when, after three exhausting days and nights, the survivors reached a line parallel with the stream of Kollaa. Behind the stream lay a series of small ridges that gave a clear view of the approaching enemy and some protection from gunfire. Communicating that a new line had been temporarily established, the phrase 'Kollaa Kestää' ('Kollaa Holds') was quickly adopted as the slogan of the war. The stubborn defence of this line stalled the Soviet juggernaut and allowed more mobile ski teams to seek out and ambush the static Soviet units. Only the sheer exhaustion of the Finnish troops caused the attacks to be suspended in late December.

Further south, the Finns could only hope to postpone the inevitable advance, and by 6 December all Finnish forces on the Karelian Isthmus were in or behind the Mannerheim Line in readiness for a major Soviet offensive. The attack opened with a 40-hour bombardment of the Finnish defences around Taipale. The Finns' defences were excavated on rising ground, affording them some protection within dugouts, but there were too few guns and not enough ammunition

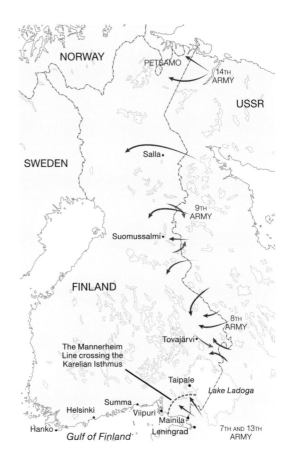

The defeat of Finland seemed to be a foregone conclusion when the Soviets invaded in 1939, but careful exploitation of the terrain, the climate, defence in depth and highly mobile troops stalled Stalin's offensives.

to indulge in counter-battery fire. Instead, as the Soviet infantry came on, Finnish artillery fired onto previously designated areas. As the Soviets continued their advance, intense small-arms fire cut down significant numbers. Astonished by the weight of fire, the Soviets fell back to their start line. For six days the Soviets attempted to get forward, but they were unable to penetrate the Mannerheim Line at any point. On 14 December, a fresh Soviet division fortified with more tanks attempted to break the Finnish defences, but it too was forced back with heavy losses. A third Soviet division renewed the assault later that same month, but the outcome was the same.

On the approach to the town of Suomussalmi on the central front, two roads could be covered by the relatively small numbers of Finnish troops. Unexpectedly, the Soviets had committed two divisions to cross the area on their way to reach Oulu, in an attempt to divide the country in half. On the Raate Road, no fewer than 14,000 Soviet troops of the 44th and 163rd Motor Rifle Divisions were strung out on the line of march when they were ambushed by the Finns. A small blocking force attacked the head of the column, while elements of the Finnish 9th Division sped around the flanks. The Finns struck at different points, forcing the Soviets into small pockets that lacked mutual support. When the Soviets tried to extract and withdraw, they were attacked over and over, causing chaos. Their regiments eventually limped out of the forests having suffered almost 9,000 casualties, while the Finns had lost no more than 400 men. Even more significant was the equipment that the Soviets had abandoned to the Fins: tanks, artillery, trucks, horses, rifles, ammunition, medical equipment and much-needed anti-tank weapons.

On the northern fronts the situation was rather different. Eight Soviet divisions had crossed the border and Petsamo had been bombarded with naval gunfire. On other coasts, however, after inflicting severe damage on the cruiser *Kirov*, Finnish shore batteries had persuaded Soviet ships to keep a safe distance. The only ally the Finns possessed here was the weather. North of the Arctic Circle, and in an exceptionally cold winter, the Finns could take advantage of perpetual darkness to conceal their movements, even in the far north where the forests gave way to tundra and open snowfields. Here the Finnish guerrilla tactics were useful in slowing, or rendering immobile, much larger Soviet formations. They tended to be well equipped for this cold weather – in contrast to the Soviet soldiers, who often had to make do with improvised shelters, inadequate clothing and indifferent leadership. To make matters worse, Soviet troops found their supply vehicles were being intercepted and attacked, and so rations were in short supply. Isolated units were sometimes deprived of food altogether. At Salla, to the northwest, a Soviet brigade was attacked on the flank by a Finnish battalion, and the Soviets retreated precipitously, leaving behind their guns and many vehicles. A Finnish counter-attack pushed the Soviets back still further and in late December 1939 the Soviets decided to abandon the northern theatre altogether because progress had been so slow.

In the southwest, where the Soviets were attempting to reach Viipuri, the Finnish defences around Summa were in danger of being breached. Despite a greater density of defensive concrete emplacements and trenches, the Soviets had located a small gap alongside the Munaso Marshes, which they exploited on 19 December. Despite this breakthrough, the Soviets had failed to support their armour, so that, as their infantry advanced, the Finns could machine gun them as before. The Soviet tanks remained isolated behind the Finnish lines and could be picked off individually. Not one armed vehicle returned to the starting point. Demoralized by the setbacks and heavy losses, some Soviet troops refused to make further futile attacks. At this point, General Harald Öhquist, the Finnish sector commander for the Karelian Isthmus, attempted to drive the Soviets back, but his counter-attack of 23 December failed. For the time being the Finns were nevertheless holding on, denying the Soviets their easy victory. In the League of Nations there was condemnation of the invasion, and Britain and France made attempts to supply the Finns with war materiel.

In January 1940, the Finns took up their encircling and ambushing raids again. The Soviets, obligingly, remained static and did not use the advantage they possessed in numbers and firepower. They were content to sit it out rather than attempt more costly attacks. The Soviets dug in their infantry and armour, using the abundance of timber to construct bunkers and reinforced trenches. The Finns quickly adapted, avoiding the strongest positions and concentrating against weaker or more demoralized formations. They also attempted to intercept airdrops intended for these static Soviet positions, further weakening the dug-in forces.

The Soviets used this pause in operations to review and make changes to their tactics and force structures. A more detailed intelligence picture was built up of the Mannerheim defences, and it was decided that all forces on the Karelian front would be organized into two armies, the 7th and 13th. Rehearsals for a major offensive were carried out against mock-up versions of the defences behind the front line. More artillery was brought up and tank formations were broken down into smaller units that could provide close support for the infantry. The original ten divisions were reinforced to 25 divisions so that 600,000 men could be brought to bear against the Finnish army. The new offensive began on 1 February 1940 with a massive concentration of artillery, stepping up a bombardment that had been continuous since December. Aerial bombing added to the devastating fire that was saturating the Finnish lines. It became impossible to move in daylight, and the Finnish troops were forced to dig deeper to escape the pulverizing effects of the Soviet guns. At night, they did what they could to repair their battered trenches. After enduring this tremendous cannonade for ten days, the Finns heard Soviet ground forces rolling forwards. Smoke screens covered their advance and the infantry and tanks this time came on together, each supporting the other. Finnish positions were being overrun, the defenders doing what they could to resist the overwhelming numbers. Astonishingly, the Finns actually managed to hold and repel the Soviets at Taipale, but in the centre a general withdrawal to the so-called Intermediate Line was ordered.

The attack had not been an outright success. Soviet casualties had been high, there was increasing pressure from the League of Nations to end the war and if the spring thaw arrived before all the military objectives were secure then the marshy terrain would add to the Soviets' difficulties. Negotiations were therefore opened, however the Soviets continued their advance, entering the ruined suburbs of Viipuri in early March. Finnish troops kept up their resistance, but ammunition supplies were limited and it seemed only a matter of time before the south was captured entirely. Despite volunteers arriving from Sweden and the other Scandinavian countries, and some military assistance from France and Britain, there was little hope of widespread foreign intervention.

To obtain peace the government of Finland agreed to the terms imposed by Moscow. Finland lost some territory, was compelled to give up about 30 per cent of its pre-war industrial resources, and almost half a million Finns were forced to evacuate the south. In addition, a Soviet military base was established at Hanko on the Gulf of Finland. The Soviets had stopped short of a full annexation. The Finns had shown every sign of fighting on, demonstrating their potential to wage an indefinite guerrilla war. The sheer determination of their troops had been enough to convince Stalin that such a war would prove too costly and humiliating. Against all odds, the Finns had taken on, and often checked, the vast Soviet steamroller, providing textbook examples of how small numbers of highly mobile and well-camouflaged forces could defeat seemingly more powerful foes.

14 /// THE BATTLE FOR THE BATAAN PENINSULA, PHILIPPINES, 1941–42

I n the Second World War, General Douglas MacArthur's defence of, and subsequent retreat into, the Bataan Peninsula in the Philippines, while plagued by tough conditions and the furious assaults of the Japanese, was a dramatic test of human endurance. The inexperienced American and Filipino forces were cut off without any hope of relief, assailed from several directions and fixed in vulnerable positions that the Japanese artillery could easily pound. When the American lines collapsed, the survivors were herded into a pocket on the peninsula and eventually, after many weeks of resistance, were taken prisoner in large numbers. Hundreds of these exhausted men were then compelled to march without respite for some 60 miles (100 km) under the bludgeoning of contemptuous guards. Any stragglers, or wounded who could go no further, were executed. The Bataan Death March (as it would come to be known) of April and May 1942 would later be judged a Japanese war crime.

Five months earlier, at precisely the same moment that Japanese aircraft swarmed over Pearl Harbor to cripple the US Pacific Fleet, a surprise attack had been unleashed on the American garrison in the Philippines. The Japanese were hoping to secure the islands rapidly in order to press further into the resource-rich Malay Archipelago of Southeast Asia. The attack began with air raids on the American bases, destroying many US planes while they were still on the ground. The raids were accompanied by landings at several locations around the Philippines by an advance guard of the Imperial Japanese 14th Army. Resistance to these landings proved difficult to coordinate, as the situation was confused and communications badly disrupted. There was, however, a spirited – if ultimately futile – series of sorties made by American pilots that damaged a number of Japanese ships and sank a minesweeper. With such minor losses, the Japanese could afford to be thorough: they spent 12 days making a detailed reconnaissance of the islands and consolidating their beachheads before the main assault forces arrived on 22 December 1941 at Lingayen Gulf in Pangasinan province, and (two days later) at Lamon Bay in Tayabas.

The initial American defensive plan was for three divisions of the Philippine Army to contain the beachheads while more deliberate operations were launched to neutralize each one. The Japanese gave no respite, however, launching themselves

Previous pages: **US soldiers on the Bataan Peninsula listen to the *Musical Mail Bag* programme, broadcast from KGEI radio station in San Francisco, 1942.**

into the assault straight off the beaches. Overwhelmed by the sheer numbers flooding ashore, and facing Japanese air superiority, the Filipino troops were quickly driven back.

MacArthur grasped the gravity of the situation immediately and initiated the pre-war defence strategy known to commanders as War Plan Orange-3. This provided for the concentration of all US and Filipino forces within Bataan and the nearby island of Corregidor, while the rest of the Philippines was abandoned in order to stabilize the situation, withstand attacks and await reinforcements from across the Pacific. MacArthur could muster 19,000 regular US troops and 11,000 Filipino soldiers. There was a nominal reserve of Filipino conscripts, but many of these deserted at the first opportunity. The chief problem was that the Pacific Fleet – on which their relief depended – had been significantly damaged at Pearl Harbor. It had previously been calculated that the Philippine garrison might be able to hold out for six months, but it was now estimated that the US armed forces would need up to two years to reassert their control of the Pacific in order to reach the islands. MacArthur and his men were on their own.

From the beachheads, Lieutenant General Masaharu Homma, the commander of Japan's 14th Army, had ordered a pincer attack to defeat the Filipino troops and next pressed on to Manila from both the north and south. With the forces of the preliminary landings also joining the advance, the Japanese overran almost the entire country in days. Manila fell on 2 January 1942. The Americans and Filipinos tried to stem the Japanese advance in order to buy time to organize the defence of the Bataan Peninsula. However, this meant fighting on unsuitable terrain for defence – as the 11th and 21st divisions discovered. They were forced to deploy in open ground and simply await the offensive. The Japanese bombarded them with artillery and airstrikes, before tanks accompanied by infantry made a ground assault. The Americans gave a good account of themselves at a terrible cost, managing to inflict significant casualties on the Japanese infantry. The problem was that each of the delaying actions was organized on a series of east–west lines (extending in depth to the south) that were easily turned on either flank. Repeatedly, the Japanese compelled the Americans to fall back to another line by utilizing a series of turning manoeuvres. For US forces, the only consolation was that the North Luzon Force, as it was styled, had enabled the South Luzon Force (the rest of the garrison) to withdraw in good order into the Bataan area.

The American defence of the peninsula was also organized into two sectors (east and west), with Mount Natib, a 4,222-foot- (1,287-m-) high peak, dividing them. A reserve of divisional strength (10,000 strong) was created to reinforce any threatened part of the perimeter. Ironically, the Japanese believed that the Philippines campaign was virtually over, and steps were taken to withdraw their 48th Division and some squadrons of aircraft while the rest of the forces were left to mop up. It therefore came as a shock to Lieutenant General Susumu Morioka, commander of the 16th Division, when his men were repulsed in an assault on the US defences around Abucay on 9 January. The Japanese had begun their attack with typical determination and fighting spirit: officers wielded samurai swords and the infantry made bayonet charges, having worked their way forwards under cover of intense fire. The Americans fought just as resolutely, making local counter-attacks to throw the Japanese back.

On 14 January, the Japanese tried again, this time attacking the US 51st Division and part of the 41st Division. They were held once more, but elements managed to slip around the flank and rear of the 51st. Japanese infantry used the valley of the Salian River to make their advance, but the movement was discovered by a foot patrol. Reinforcements rushed to fill the gap and a close-quarter battle broke out that resulted in a Japanese tactical withdrawal. Further east, a similar infiltration along the Abo-Abo Valley proved more successful. Under pressure from in front and behind, the American line collapsed and reinforcements had to rush to plug the breach. In the close country, establishing a coherent 'front line' was problematic, and consequently the fighting was intense.

The next day, the Japanese again penetrated the lines of the American forces, exploiting the relatively undefended slopes of Mount Natib. They established posts on the Mauban Ridge and beat off the desperate counter-attacks of two US divisions. Further Japanese night attacks and infiltrations brought them into the American rear areas, and later in January the decision was taken to abandon the peninsula's first line of defence. As the frontline elements tried to extract along a route known as Trail 2 they were assaulted, and it took a hastily organized defensive action to stem the Japanese attack. While the main assault was checked, a detachment of Japanese infantry, perhaps 2,000 strong, succeeded in getting behind the US lines via the valleys of the Tuol River and the Gogo-Cotar River. To eliminate these elements, a series of attacks was made by American troops between

23 January and 17 February – an action known as the Battle of the Pockets. The fighting was particularly savage, even by the standards of the campaign, and it is thought that perhaps as few as 377 Japanese soldiers escaped to their own lines. The fighting had thus far left both sides exhausted, and Homma ordered a pause in the offensive to reorganize. The brief suspension of Japanese attacks allowed the Americans to reoccupy some of the ground lost and to restructure their own defences.

To regain the initiative, the Japanese made amphibious landings on the west coast of the Bataan Peninsula on 22 January 1942. The Americans managed seriously to disrupt these plans when a pair of motorboats intercepted the Japanese during the landings: two barges were sunk and the rest scattered up and down the coast. The Japanese were now divided and had to try to consolidate their beachheads. The only personnel available to resist the landing force were men of the Philippine Constabulary, a single US infantry battalion, some aircrew and sailors, and marines from an anti-aircraft battery near by. In reaction to the new threat, some machine guns were removed from aircraft and mounted on specially built platforms, while the sailors attempted to stain their white uniforms khaki to blend in with the local countryside. Counter-attacks were ordered, and the Japanese troops were

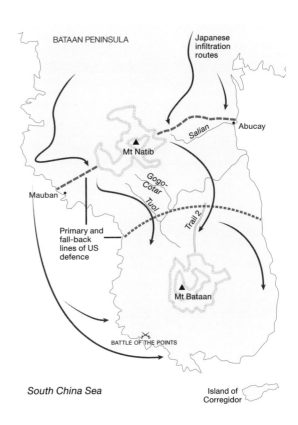

The American and Filipino garrisons were overwhelmed by a series of Japanese thrusts from several directions. Cut off, and without hope of relief, the Americans nevertheless held on to the Bataan Peninsula, and defeated a series of attacks.

unable to break out of their perimeters. The ensuing firefights, later known as the Battle of the Points, were as close-fought as any of the campaign. Eventually the Japanese (who had numbered perhaps 2,000) were entirely wiped out, save for a handful of survivors who escaped to their own lines. It took the troops three weeks to regain control of these beaches.

The fighting continued to drag on for some weeks before the Japanese commanders realized they needed to reinforce 14th Army and make a final attempt to destroy the American garrison on Bataan. Throughout March, a variety of heavy guns, including monster 240 mm howitzers, were brought in. By 3 April, 300 guns had been assembled to pulverize American dugouts, and Japanese bombers added to the storm of fire. Foliage was stripped from the trees and soil and rock were blasted into the air. After the bombardment, Japanese infantry and armour began to drive forward, systematically working their way into and through each position over three days. The entire American and Filipino line was driven back and Homma brought forward his plans for the final annihilation of the defenders. Flanking attacks were successful and a thrust into the centre of the American line penetrated deeply enough to reach all of its objectives. Anticipating counter-attacks, the Japanese positioned themselves to receive them and inflicted predictably heavy losses. When the American and Filipino reserves were committed, they failed to hold any of the ground that they had retaken. American communications broke down, and units began to fall back in a disorganized way.

The American and Filipino forces were now close to collapse. They had resisted without external supplies for over three months and were tired, hungry and outfought on every front. There seemed to be a collective realization that the game was up. Major General Edward King organized negotiations in order to save his men from complete destruction, although Corregidor held out for another month. Overall, the efforts of the beleaguered 'Battling Bastards of Bataan' had cost the Japanese time, effort and lives by disrupting their plans for the swift conquest of Southeast Asia. Perhaps most important was the sense of moral victory. Although taken by surprise, the Americans had not yielded, even when their position was hopeless. They had defied the Japanese and exhibited a determination that was to characterize the entire American Pacific campaign. The ensuing mistreatment of American and Filipino prisoners during the Bataan Death March deepened a sense of disgust for their adversary that galvanized resistance.

MacArthur had evacuated from Bataan before it fell to the Japanese in 1942, vowing to return. He did so, along with an American task force, and retook Bataan on 8 February 1945. Nevertheless, the Japanese continued to fight in other parts of the Pacific theatre with extraordinary courage and tenacity. Many of their troops willingly sacrificed themselves to save their country, their Emperor and their honour. Despite this, the Japanese imperialist mission seemed doomed to failure against the sheer scale of American power, and had even faltered in the Philippines faced with the grit and determination of American servicemen and their allies, stranded without resources, hope of relief or a place to run. We should not ignore the fact that the fall of Bataan was a defeat, and the mistreatment of those taken into captivity reinforced the sense of humiliation that had first stung the Americans at Pearl Harbor. The resolve to recover the Philippines was driven by the desire to avenge the defeat of 1942 and to reassert American supremacy in the Pacific. There had been only one redeeming feature in the action in the Philippines: the American troops at Bataan had battled on against all odds knowing they were merely staving off the inevitable, but their spirit had inspired respect and set the standard for the fighting in the future.

The final broadcast from the Philippines before its fall summed up that spirit: 'The world will long remember the epic struggle that Filipino and American soldiers put up in the jungle fastness and along the rugged coast of Bataan. They have stood up uncomplaining under the constant and grueling fire of the enemy for more than three months. Besieged on land and blockaded by sea, cut off from all sources of help in the Philippines and in America, the intrepid fighters have done all that human endurance could bear.'

T he desperate Soviet defence of Stalingrad, often by only a few handfuls of soldiers in different locations, brought the seemingly irresistible Nazi expansion in Europe to a standstill. Even today it is difficult to grasp the vast scale of this battle. What made it a particularly grim struggle was not just the sheer number of losses, but the fact that men were compelled to fight among the ruins of a modern urban environment in bitter weather. Familiar landscapes were rendered into an alien world of twisted metal, shattered buildings and blasted concrete slabs. The battle was fought as intensely below the ground as it was on the surface, and a vicious struggle for air supremacy was waged throughout the engagement. Yet, despite the modern setting of this battle, it was the timeless endurance and courage of the individual soldiers that characterized the conflict. Single streets, even isolated buildings, became the scenes of struggles out of all proportion to their tactical or strategic value. This was a battle that demanded a rugged ruthlessness in order to ensure one's survival, but even then the odds of living through Stalingrad were extremely low.

Hitler's invasion of the Soviet Union in June 1941, code-named Operation Barbarossa, swept so swiftly through Eastern Europe that it seemed only a matter of time before their enemies there collapsed. The German blitzkrieg had been successful in Poland, France, the Low Countries and the Balkans; it now drove on through the Ukraine towards Russia, periodically encircling or destroying larger formations. By the end of the year the Nazis were nearing the outskirts of Moscow and Leningrad, while, to the south, they had cut off the Crimea and secured the Don River. During the winter, Soviet counter-attacks had been contained and defeated, their only success being a vast offensive outside Moscow, but even this resulted in fearful losses.

As a result, Hitler began to contemplate finishing off the Soviets and securing the resources of the region. Plans were drawn up that involved the cold-blooded purging of (particularly Jewish) local populations, the exploitation of the grain-producing areas, and the seizing of industrial plants. Above all, Hitler wanted to bring to an end any threat of shortages – especially oil shortages – within his growing empire. This meant concentrating a portion of his armed forces (Army Group South) on the capture of the Caucasus, and from there driving on into Iraq

Previous pages A Soviet soldier in the ruined city maintains a stubborn resistance, January 1943.

and the Persian Gulf. Although a limited number of Allied forces had previously invaded Iraq and Iran to thwart pro-Nazi plots, Hitler was close to his goal. Army Group South was to be divided into two wings to fulfil its mission of taking the oilfields of the southern USSR. Army Group A was to head southeast along the smaller local roads, while Army Group B protected the northern flank of this thrust by pushing towards the Volga River.

Army Group B, led by General Friedrich von Paulus, was ordered to sever the Soviet line of communication that ran north–south along the river. The mighty waterway of the Volga was an economic artery that could be used to shift tons of war materiel to the centre and north of the country. The largest city and river port on the Volga was Stalingrad, so-named because of the Soviet leader's defence there during the Russian Civil War. If this city fell, the Soviet defence of Western Russia would be completely unhinged. In Hitler's mind, the Volga also marked the easternmost boundary of his imagined empire. He had written in his autobiography, *Mein Kampf,* how National Socialists would hone their fighting skills on this frontier in order to develop the right character before taking their place as full citizens of the Third Reich in Germany.

The German offensive against Stalingrad was delayed by the stubborn defence at the port of Sebastopol in the Crimea and then by confusion over the composition of Army Groups A and B, which led to a tremendous traffic jam. Once prepared, though, the Germans took crossings over the Don and drove the Soviets back towards the Volga as planned. In summer 1942, Stalingrad was subjected to the largest air raid of the war to date, while a pincer movement brought the Germans to the banks of the river to the north and south. In autumn, somewhat delayed, the first units began to fight their way into the city outskirts.

The initial defence of the city depended on a relatively small number of men and women, including all-female anti-aircraft batteries that used their guns against tanks as well as planes. Although they lacked training in ground combat, the women levelled their guns and fought with great determination against the battle-hardened *Wehrmacht*. The Germans were astonished to find they were fighting women, but even more surprised that they had to wipe out every single detachment before they could get through the city. Factory workers also mounted a hasty defence while keeping the production lines running. With shells exploding around them, the men and women of the city's tank factory were especially keen to stay in action. As each new T-34 was completed it was driven, unpainted and only partially armed, straight into the battle line.

The Soviets had been reinforced by Lieutenant General Vasily Chuikov, who (under the regional direction of Marshal Andrei Yeryomenko) also now led the resistance. They continued to strengthen their defence by ferrying thousands of men west across the Volga to the city. Every boat and barge was subject to heavy fire as the Germans employed artillery and mortars, or exploited their air superiority and made stuka dive-bombing attacks. The howling of these aircraft and the whistling of their bombs were a terrifying experience for the men packed into vulnerable little craft. Despite attempts to protect them with anti-aircraft fire from the banks, hundreds were killed. To prevent the soldiers from diving into the water to escape, specially selected guards lined the bulwarks with orders to shoot anyone who made the attempt. Similar instructions were given once ashore to stop those who attempted to fall back during the street fighting. The orders were often fulfilled by these special guards (perhaps fearful of their own destruction) with ruthless efficiency.

It was expected that Soviet soldiers would fight or die for each and every yard of Stalingrad. Similarly, German troops were exhorted to exhibit a National Socialist ardour, and impose their

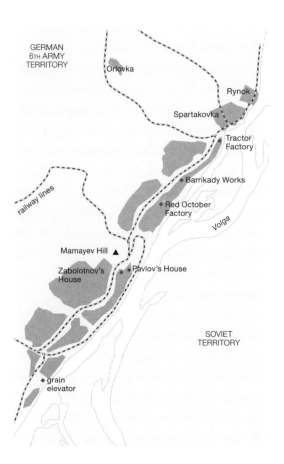

The Soviet troops, although subjected to ceaseless air and ground attack, and with their only – precarious – supply line across the Volga River, held on to every block, every street, every building and every room with fierce determination.

will over inferior Slavic *Untermenschen* (subhumans). Since the beginnings of the campaign in 1941, there had been a callous disregard for enemy personnel, and – all too often – prisoners were routinely executed. The Nazi high command was particularly keen to inflict casualties to hasten *Vernichtung* (annihilation) of the Russians, which in their eyes would advance the racial cleansing of Eastern Europe.

Hitherto, the German army had been able to make efficient use of its advantage in tactics and doctrine. The emphasis was on combined arms operations: coordinating air power, artillery, armour and infantry to inflict a decisive defeat on their enemies. Yet in the urban environment it proved far more difficult to make effective use of their indirect fire assets. Essentially, the Germans had to bombard an area before making a limited advance with infantry supported by small numbers of tanks and armoured personnel carriers (APCs). The Soviets learnt to draw the Germans into prepared 'killing zones', make ambushes with multiple firing points, or use hit-and-run tactics. They fought from buildings, sewers and basements. When the Germans demolished houses and factories with their gunfire, the Soviets would reoccupy the ruins and turn them into new defences. Some streets evoked apocalyptic cityscapes, filled with piles of rubble that acted as ready-made anti-tank barriers. The unburied dead lay amid these ruins, adding to the horror of the scene.

By 27 September, the Germans had secured 90 per cent of the city, and had cut the areas held by the defenders into two pockets. The zones still held by the Soviets measured no more than a few hundred metres square each, and this allowed the Germans to concentrate their gunfire. Crucially, the German observation point on Mamayev Hill meant that accurate artillery fire could be brought down every time the Soviets sent men across the river. Some vessels received a direct hit and their troops were killed instantly, while others were riddled with shrapnel and deluged with gallons of freezing water thrown up by the explosions. Those who survived the crossing were sheltered briefly by river bluffs, but were then pitched into the battle for survival. By the first week of October, the Soviet 62nd Army was in theory 100,000 strong, but actually numbered only 53,000 and was reported to have suffered 80,000 casualties in just one month: despite the constant flow of reinforcements and replacements, the Soviets were haemorrhaging the lives of their men in the defence of the city.

In the city centre, however, small detachments were continuing to fight for every yard of ground. A platoon under Lieutenant Afanasev took over a large complex of buildings just 300 yards (275 m) from the river and fortified them. Afanasev was blinded soon after and he handed command to his senior non-commissioned officer, Sergeant Yakov Pavlov. Pavlov's detachment moved into a four-storey house overlooking a road junction and an open space beyond. In the basement were sheltering civilians, some of whom joined the defence. Soon, successive waves of German infantry, often supported by armour, attempted to cross this open area as they approached the building. Every time they did so, Pavlov's men opened up from the windows of each storey, attacking the Germans with concentrated machine-gun fire. Casualties were heavy. The German response was to intensify the barrage against the structure, but Pavlov's men would shelter from the worst bombardments in the basements, which they connected by knocking through the walls. Certain rooms in the upper levels were turned into small fortresses and bunkers, with loop-holed walls to allow fire. The Soviet soldiers clung to the building as their only means of survival, for each man knew that to retreat would mean execution by their own secret police or political commissars. Surrender to the Germans was also out of the question, since, even if they were not killed immediately, thousands were dying of starvation or mistreatment in prisoner-of-war camps. Their only hope lay in fighting and killing the Germans as fast as they could. According to one account, small sorties had to be made after German attacks in order to drag away the bodies so as to clear the fields of fire for the machine guns.

In another part of the city centre, Lieutenant Zabolotnov and a small group of Soviet soldiers from the remnants of the 42nd Regiment took over a building in Solmechnaya Street. They worked to fortify the structure and even though Zabolotnov was killed, his name was given to the house by successive waves of Soviet fighters. A German officer noted that: 'For every house, workshop, water tower, railway embankment, wall, cellar and every pile of ruins, a bitter battle was waged, without equal even in the First World War with its vast expenditure of munitions.' When German troops attempted to capture a grain elevator in the southern part of the city, it took days of intense fighting and hundreds of men to gain a foothold beneath it, and then to fight through it. After the position was finally taken, only 40 Soviet soldiers were found to have occupied it. Small squads – half a dozen at a time – were despatched by Soviet headquarters to fight in the sewers, or to infiltrate the German lines and pour fire into the rear of any attack. The Germans complained of these 'gangster methods', and used artillery in a close support role to demolish yet more of the city, but the Soviets only reoccupied the ruins and used the acres of twisted metal in the factory districts to conceal their anti-tank weapons, machine guns and snipers.

Having swept through the village of Orlovka to the north, and punched through to the banks of the Volga in the centre of Stalingrad, the German VIth Army turned its attention to both reducing the Soviet hold on the southern part of the city centre and squeezing out the last remaining salient in the northern factory district alongside the river. There were five key positions where resistance was strongest: the Red October Factory, the Barrikady Works, the Dzerzhinsky Tractor Factory and the residential areas of Spartakovka and Rynok. On 30 September, aware that an assault against the factories was imminent, the Soviets attempted to disrupt their opponents by making a counter-attack on the eve of the German attack. In confused fighting, the Germans nevertheless seemed to gain the upper hand by daybreak. The Soviet division led by General Smikhotvorov was reduced from 15,000 men to 2,000 in a week. Soviet battalions, theoretically 1000 strong, were reduced to handfuls of fugitives.

On 3 October, the Germans made their attack against the Red October Factory, with three infantry divisions and two panzer divisions channelled into a front only 3 miles (5 km) wide. Soviet reinforcements were rushed in, sometimes so precipitously that they arrived without headquarter elements, tanks or anti-tank weapons. The men fought desperately and halted the German attack, checking a similar thrust against the Tractor Factory the following day. By nightfall the Germans had lost four battalions and secured only a single block of flats. On 13 October, the Soviets made a major counter-attack at the Tractor Factory, but retook only a few hundred yards of street. The losses they had taken in return nearly crippled their defence. The following day the Germans made a massive air raid – the Luftwaffe recorded 3,000 sorties – against the factory area and German artillery pulverized the zone so fiercely that smoke and dust were suspended in the air, reducing visibility to 100 yards (90 m). By 1130 hours, 180 tanks had burst through the Soviet lines in the Tractor Factory, and by 1600 hours the garrison there was completely encircled – though still fighting. At midnight, fighting was still continuous and every workshop was being contested. Production lines became the scenes of murderous firefights. In 48 hours, 5,000 men were killed or wounded in the battle for this single complex.

The Germans managed to capture the Tractor Factory on 15 October, although just to the north pockets of Soviet soldiers continued to fight on, and a handful of Soviet guns and aircraft still showered the Germans with every shell and bomb they could lay their hands on. The Soviet defenders had lost 13,000 men in a week's fighting and were pressed back into an even smaller area, but they continued to deny the city to their enemies. The western end of the Red October Factory was in German hands, as was part of the Barrikady Works, but elsewhere the resistance went on. On 20 October, the gallant defenders at Pavlov's house managed to knock out a column of four panzers and scatter their infantry support. The little garrison held out for a total of 58 days. The Soviets were holding on against the odds.

Slowly the Germans were being bled and drawn into a trap. Attrition rates for German units were so alarming that reinforcements were being sucked in from surrounding formations. Moreover, slowly but surely the Soviets were ensuring they gained greater control of the skies. The loss of Luftwaffe air superiority was never absolute, but the airspace could no longer be used with impunity as in the past. Towards the end of October, German assaults started to peter out due to exhaustion, lack of ammunition and catastrophic losses. Massed artillery across the Volga also reduced the Germans' ability to advance any further. Soviet Katyusha rocket salvos arrived suddenly, and in a barrage that covered a wide area. By the time troops tried to take cover, the devastation was already complete. In one instance, an entire German battalion was destroyed by a single rocket attack. The Germans nevertheless continued to strike as best they could. When winter weather arrived in November, they intensified their fire against the Soviets' river crossings, knowing that with ice floes and blizzard conditions, they could significantly add to their adversaries' hardships.

The Soviets then executed Operation Uranus, a brilliant encirclement. On 19 November, having completely retained the element of surprise, they unleashed a tremendous bombardment on the lines held by Axis armies north and south of the city. Entire army groups had been carefully and secretly built up while the Stalingrad battle raged and were now speeding across the crumbling German lines, catching the main body of men in a pincer move. In ten days, the German VIth Army had been cut off entirely. Jubilant Soviet troops from north and south met near Kalach to the west of Stalingrad, relieved that the crisis had passed and that they, at last, had returned to the offensive. It was to be many weeks before the

Germans could be pushed further west, and it took days of bitter fighting to seal off and cut down the Germans in the 'cauldron' pocket. Eventually, the German garrison was starved out, and on the last day of January 1943 they capitulated. Emerging from bunkers and dugouts in the snow, the Germans were bundled up in every conceivable item of clothing to keep out the cold. The Soviets were aware that they had brought about a turning point in the war, although it had come at a terrible cost: it is estimated that some three million perished in the slaughter at Stalingrad. Nevertheless, the Soviets had demonstrated that, whatever the odds against them, they had fought on undeterred.

16 /// THE DEFENCE OF KOHIMA, BURMA–INDIA BORDER, 1944

*T*he Allied defence of Kohima from 4 April to 22 June 1944 during the Second
World War involved battles across a tennis court, intense trench fighting
and inspirational courage. It was the ultimate close-quarter battle, fought
by an outnumbered British and Indian garrison and a highly motivated
Japanese army. Kohima marked the high tide of Japanese military expansion. Over the
course of three years, the Imperial Japanese Army had swept British, American,
Dutch, French and Southeast Asian forces before them, and had earned a reputation
for invincibility.

The Imperial Japanese forces were characterized by courageous frontal
assaults regardless of casualties, ritual suicides to avoid capture and defensive
battles contested to the death. They were, however, also condemned for 'illegal'
ruses of war, including booby traps and ambushes, as well as suicide attacks,
such as human mines and kamikaze aircraft. At the time the West gave the explan-
ation that this was all just 'fanaticism', but this was really an excuse to avoid the
thorough analysis of a formidable and determined adversary. In Japanese military
culture, many old martial traditions remained embedded in training and doctrine.
A rigid form of militarism, derived from ideas of self-discipline in martial arts,
reinforced military values as a means of both unifying Japanese people, and provided a framework for their daily thought. Japanese soldiers were inculcated with
values that emphasized utter obedience to the Emperor, his officers and all their
orders; these values also encouraged self-deprivation, sacrifice, faith, comrade-
ship, physical courage, honour and the desire to atone for shame or failure. Each
man was taught to take the view that death, while not necessarily imminent, was
inevitable and therefore ought to be accepted quietly whatever the circumstances
in which it was presented. Even civilians faithfully recited the military slogan:
'Duty is weightier than a mountain, while death is lighter than a feather.' In the
army there was a strong culture of competition, driving soldiers to excel against
all others and to regard all non-Japanese as inferior, and therefore deserving
of defeat.

By the outbreak of the Pacific War in 1941, these philosophical values had
been developed into the *Senjinkun* (soldier's code). In it, duty was elevated to a religious mission. The army, soldiers were told, was the means of bringing about

Previous pages: The 'lunar landscape' of the Battle of Kohima, 1944.

Hakkō Ichi-U (ultimate world unity). Obedience to the Emperor in this endeavour was vital because he was, they believed, a deity. His orders could not be disobeyed since they were religious instructions. Consequently, failure in battle meant a soldier let down not just his comrades, but also the country, the Emperor and the divine mission. The only way to atone for this failure or prevent the situation getting worse was to remove oneself from the mission honourably, that is by *seppuku* (ritual suicide). The code demanded that enemies were to be treated courteously only if they had behaved honourably: those that surrendered disgraced themselves. The courage of the Japanese in battle was, however, only in part due to this idea of a mission – it was also closely connected to Shintoism. Soldiers who had fallen in battle were deified at the Yasukuni shrine in Tokyo, and it was a widely held belief that they would be immediately transmitted to paradise, where they would enjoy immortality among the gods.

During training, the Japanese soldiers received religious instruction along-side their military tutorial. The *seishin kyōiku* were a set of religious values or virtues closely tied to the Senjinkun. These values were reinforced constantly through battlefield tours, slogans in mess halls, lectures and visits to museums. From these precepts, the soldiers were expected to cultivate a sense of inner power (the *kiai*) that united the mind and the will to form an irresistible force. Developing kiai required gruelling training: recruits were beaten for the first few days after arrival to toughen them; there were marches of 50 miles (80 km); tests of endurance; and a spartan lifestyle. A day's rations, for example, consisted of two portions of milled rice and three servings of tea – the rest was down to improvisation and initiative. The training regime included a strong emphasis on bayonets. As in the West, they were attributed with a moral as well as physical value. Because of the bayonet's association with close-quarter fighting, it was thought to embody the 'spirit' of the attack. Indeed, the Japanese Army was taught that the bayonet charge was always the climax of the assault, and it was thought to foster aggression in each individual. This may explain why, even when Japanese forces faced defeat in the latter stages of the Battle of Kohima, they would attempt to make a final bayonet charge. It was the attitude that made them such formidable opponents. General Hideki Tōjō, the commander of Japanese forces, ordered his troops to fight to extermination, or kill themselves if they failed in their mission.

The Japanese infantry were also taught that infiltration using all the available terrain and rapid movement was preferable to a frontal assault. In a number of battles throughout 1942 and 1943 the Japanese had demonstrated their skill in moving even large formations in this way, encircling the British using jungle tracks, or driving deep behind their lines. But the British had also learnt to adapt to these tactics, and by 1944 they had built up their forces and improved training. There was better coordination between formations, a greater abundance of air power and artillery, as well as more efficient supply systems. Although the terrain lent itself to the envelopment of enemies, the British learnt to fight on even if surrounded, with each unit in a self-contained box formation. In addition, they decided to play the Japanese at their own game and deployed thousands of Chindits (highly trained jungle troops) behind Japanese lines to attack their logistics and disrupt their plans.

After the fall of Singapore in 1942, the British and Indian forces were driven back through Burma at the height of the monsoon, and British efforts to contain or defeat the Japanese the following year remained unsuccessful. In the spring of 1944, the Japanese launched the U Go Offensive across the border of India, initially intending to disrupt the concentration of the Indian Army IV Corps at Imphal. Lieutenant General Renya Mutaguchi, commander of the Japanese 15th Army, believed that if sufficient determination was shown by all ranks, there was the opportunity to break the British resistance in the region once and for all. Plans were therefore drawn up to push into India, and to send the 31st Division to seize Kohima and cut off the routes to Imphal. From Kohima, the division would press on to Dimapur, the main logistics base for the Indian Army in the area. In fact the commander of 31st Division, Lieutenant General Kōtoku Satō, had grave misgivings about the plan and believed that his logistical system would break down under the strain.

On 15 March 1944, Satō's division crossed the Chindwin River at Homalin and then wound its way along jungle trails until it clashed with elements of the Indian Army covering the northern approaches to Imphal just five days later. The commander of the Japanese 58th Regiment was aware that the Indian 50th Parachute Brigade in front of him at Sangshak was not his primary objective, but he nevertheless resolved to drive them off in order to take the initiative in the campaign. The Japanese must have had some misgivings when it took six days of intense fighting to dislodge the Indian troops. In fact, only when artillery and reinforcements from the 15th Division arrived could the Japanese be certain of success. They had inflicted 600 casualties and overrun the British Indian Army positions, but the whole enterprise had taken up a week, and thus delayed the main offensive.

The intensity of the fighting had alerted Lieutenant General (later Field Marshal) Bill Slim, the British commander of Fourteenth Army, to the scale and direction of the Japanese offensive. It had been widely believed that the terrain and close vegetation would prevent the Japanese making any thrust towards Kohima with a force any larger than a regiment (the equivalent of a British brigade) and consequently it was only lightly held. Steps were soon underway, however, to reinforce Imphal. The 5th Indian Division was flown in from Arakan, where it had just defeated the Japanese at the Battle of the Admin Box. Elements of other units were flown or transported by rail to Dimapur. These included the 23rd Long Range Penetration Brigade of the famous Chindits, whose task it was to harass the right flank of any Japanese advance.

The Kohima ridge feature dominated the road that led from

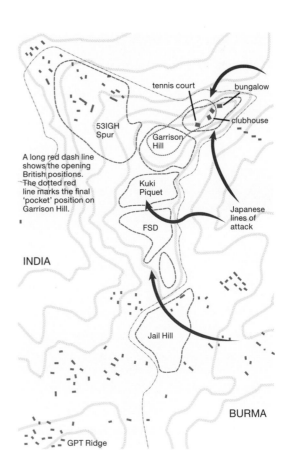

Surrounded, fighting daily at close quarters and practically overwhelmed, the small garrison of Kohima held up the Japanese offensive into India with inspirational courage and determination. Their effort helped turn the tide of the war in Southeast Asia.

Dimapur to the three British divisions holding Imphal, and it was clear that if the Japanese were able to capture this position then the way into India would be open. The settlement at Kohima was also the administrative centre of Nagaland in north-east India, and on the ridge itself stood the Deputy Commissioner's bungalow, with clubhouses and a tennis court on the terraces above. Many of the slopes were covered in thick vegetation, so the ridge was hardly ideal for defence. To the north of the ridge lay a settlement known as Naga Village, dominated by two features known as Treasury Hill and Church Knoll, while to the south lay two more areas of high ground called GPT Ridge and Aradura Spur. Along the main ridge, local units had labelled their positions as Garrison Hill, Kuki Piquet, 53IGH Spur and FSD. In front of the position, to the east, men of the local Assam Regiment were ordered to make a delaying action.

On 1 April, the leading formations of the Japanese 31st Division made contact with the Assamese picquets and quickly overran them, bundling the surviving troops back towards Naga Village. The Japanese then made a reconnaissance of the ridge, and began concentrating their units to the north and south. While the 4th Battalion, the Queen's Own Royal West Kent Regiment took up defensive positions along the ridge, the rest of their brigade soon found itself cut off by a Japanese thrust to the west of the ridge that had cut the road. This meant that the Shere Battalion (an inexperienced unit from Nepal), logisticians and some troops of the Burmese Regiment made up a garrison on the Kohima Ridge. In total there were no more than 2,500 men – with this number including around 1,000 non-combatant personnel.

On 6 April, the Japanese began what they thought was the final assault on the ridge, firing artillery and mortars with such intensity that the garrison was soon driven into a pocket on Garrison Hill. Continuous shelling blasted the vegetation away and smashed tree trunks to matchwood. Worse, it was found that unprotected supplies of water had been left on GPT Ridge, which had since fallen into Japanese hands. The sole water supply now available to the defending force was a small spring on Garrison Hill that could be reached only at night. Its slow trickle meant that obtaining a few gallons took hours. As the Japanese flanked to the south of Garrison Hill, the dressing stations for wounded men were exposed to gunfire, and, as a result a number of wounded men were hit a second time. Unburied and muti-lated remains littered the battlefield.

At the north end of the ridge, the situation was just as serious. Working their way forward, the Japanese managed to get within a few yards of the Deputy Commissioner's bungalow. There they were halted by a determined defence that forced them to dig in alongside the tennis court, while the British manned their trenches and foxholes opposite. Grenades were hurled into enemy positions and snipers attempted to cut down anyone exposed on the surface – British soldiers taking combat supplies to forward positions were especially at risk, and had to crawl to avoid sniper fire.

Before long, the British soldiers would hear the voices of their adversaries forming up out of sight in the gathering darkness. Fire support would be called for, to smash the Japanese at their forming up points, but the furious attacks would always come anyway with infantrymen yelling, gunfire pouring in. The British troops would reply with long bursts of Bren gun fire, a shower of grenades 'like cricket balls' (as one eyewitness described) and rifle fire at the 'rapid' rate. The Japanese infantrymen would crumple, fall or be tossed backwards by high velocity rounds and then their attack would waver and fall back. There would be a pause while the Japanese regrouped, then they might try to infiltrate, crawling forward until practically on top of the position, or they might mount another impetuous charge. The Bren guns glowed red after each attack in the darkness, and, after the relief of finding oneself still alive, then began the business of restocking ammunition, pulling the wounded out of the firing line, replacing the killed men, or taking shelter from the renewed Japanese shellfire that followed every assault. Assamese and Punjabi soldiers also took their turn at the centre of the line, absorbing Japanese artillery and mortar fire, and repelling infantry assaults with the same desperate determination.

Airdrops could sometimes bring precious relief, particularly water, medical supplies, grenades and ammunition, but some drops missed their targets and fell into Japanese hands. Snipers shot down those attempting to retrieve canisters suspended by their parachutes from the trees. Water containers were riddled by Japanese gunners before they could be secured.

On 14 April, Colonel Hugh Richards, the commander of the Kohima garrison, made an Order of the Day that was distributed to every sub-unit of the survivors. It gave simple praise to the men for their endurance and deplored the suffering of the wounded. There was a hint that relief might soon come. It concluded with the words: 'put your trust in God and continue to hit the enemy hard wherever he may show himself. If you do that, his defeat is sure.'

On 17 April, after ten days of fighting, the Japanese made one more gigantic effort to blast the British and their Indian allies from the ridge. They swarmed over the tennis court and secured the bungalow, before readying themselves for the final assault on Garrison Hill. The situation was desperate for the British Indian Army. Positions everywhere seemed to be falling to overwhelming numbers; platoons were in some cases reduced to three men; in one platoon every single man had been wounded at least once. So many had been killed or wounded that further resistance seemed hopeless. Only one of the Royal West Kent's mortar sections remained in action. Sergeant King, the battalion's commander, had had his jaw broken by a shell fragment, yet kept his team in action, holding his broken and bleeding face as he did so. Alongside the high explosive, the Japanese fired in phosphorous shells – their terrifying white tendrils of burning chemicals arcing across the hillsides, leaving noxious smoke to conceal the jogging infantry behind. But the survivors refused to give way. Kuki Piquet was captured, which cut the British garrison in two, but still they held on. The British now occupied an area of only 350 square yards (290 square metres). Everyone waited for the next dawn, knowing it could be the day the Japanese fought their way to the summit.

Yet instead of a final attack, the British suddenly received reinforcements from the 161st Brigade, which itself had been relieved by the breakthrough of the 2nd Division. The brigade had to fight their way in, but the air, artillery and armoured support began to turn the tide. The relieving forces advanced across a lunar landscape of craters and trenches, and evacuated the wounded under cover of darkness – still subjected to intense fire even then. By 20 April, the original garrison had been replaced by the British 6th Brigade but, despite this success, the Japanese were still numerically superior and undaunted in their determination to seize the ridge. Several Japanese charges were made against Garrison Hill, and there were recurring episodes of hand-to-hand combat. Kuki Piquet remained in Japanese hands, spanning the ridgeline, but on the northern side of Garrison Hill the situation was changing. During a night attack on 26 April 1944, the British managed to retake the clubhouse above the Deputy Commissioner's bungalow and this allowed them to look down into the Japanese positions below. A concentration of howitzers, field guns and two 5.5 inch medium guns had supported the attack, as had the RAF, and while this undoubtedly helped to keep Japanese reinforcements pinned down, the British infantry still had to fight for every foxhole and bunker with grenades, rifles and bayonets. The Japanese had spent time deepening and concealing their positions, so that gun slits could be opened and closed. If the British tried to assault through one position, they were immediately caught in the crossfire of others. It was an impossible situation.

Attempts were made to catch the Japanese in a pincer by attacking both extreme flanks north and south. The monsoon rains made progress even more difficult. The soil, when cleared of vegetation, degenerated into a glutinous ooze of cloying mud. Elsewhere, pounding rain turned slopes into treacherous and slippery ramps. Even where British forces could get forward and gain a small foothold, as in the Naga Village, Japanese counter-attacks could still drive them out. In the south, GPT Ridge was taken in a surprise British attack, but it proved impossible to capture the entire position in one go, and so a see-saw struggle of bitter close-quarter fighting continued after the initial success. Taking a single hill or ridge back from the Japanese became an epic.

It required a week of intense fighting and heavy casualties to recapture Jail Hill, not least because the Japanese had dug in machine guns on the reverse slope of GPT Ridge that could target any attackers as they scaled the adjacent hill feature. As each of the ridges fell, only Japanese entrenched in the tennis court and garden below the Deputy Commissioner's bungalow held out. On 13 May, the British used a bulldozer to drive a new track to the summit, and up this soldiers hauled a single tank. The tank went into action alongside the 2nd Battalion, the Dorsetshire Regiment; together they blasted each Japanese position in turn at point blank range. It was a curious finale to the battle: a tank firing its main armament into the apertures of one of the most confined battlefields in the world. Wreathed in the smoke of the smouldering bunkers were the sweating, muddy and exhausted British troops in their drab olive-green uniforms. They were tired, but relieved that, at last, the Kohima Ridge was theirs again. Nearby, looking alertly over the parapets they had hastily constructed, were the Indian troops of the 33rd Infantry Brigade – men who had fought for every yard of the Kuki Piquet and the FSD and DIS ridges.

On 12 May, Naga Village had also been attacked but it was not until the 16th that it was finally cleared. The Japanese troops were determined to fight on, but – as Satō had feared – their logistical system had broken down entirely. British special forces were operating on the Japanese right flank, harassing them, while the RAF did their best to disrupt Japanese resupply efforts. The Japanese were also pursuing too many objectives, and it was not clear whether Imphal or Kohima was the main target. The Japanese withdrawal from the Kohima area began on 1 June, when their supply situation had entirely collapsed. The British began to push their assailants further back, and the forces from Kohima and Imphal linked up on 22 June.

Some 4,064 British and Indian troops had been killed at Kohima, but they had inflicted losses of over 5,700 on the Japanese. More importantly, they had broken the mystique of the Japanese soldier. British and Indian troops still respected them, but the Imperial Japanese opponent was no longer a superman able to live off the jungle and strike with impunity from every direction. The Allies at Kohima had proved that the Japanese could be beaten, and decisively. The special forces teams had shown that they could match the Japanese in their jungle skills and ability to infiltrate enemy lines. The British and Indian soldiers had demonstrated they too could take heavy losses, make spirited attacks and sweep their enemy from their positions. Strategically, the losses the Japanese suffered, physical as well as psychological, meant the stage was set for the liberation of Burma and Southeast Asia. It took less than two years to drive the Japanese back to southern Burma and retake Rangoon, all the while inflicting a series of crippling defeats on them. While the Pacific War ended with the use of atomic weapons against the Japanese mainland, we should not forget that Southeast Asia was retaken the old-fashioned way, with the right tactics, sound logistics, sheer guts and determination.

Field Marshal Slim, Commander 14th Army, later wrote: 'Sieges have been longer, but few have been more intense, and in none have the defenders deserved greater honour than the garrison of Kohima.' Kohima was the turning point in the Burma campaign. If the ridge had been lost, the route to India would have been open and the situation for the Indian Army would have been critical. The defence of the ridge broke the tide of Japanese expansion, wrecked their ability to rely on movement to maintain their supplies, forced them onto the defensive and smashed the myth of their invincibility. A simple memorial was erected to commemorate the efforts of the British 2nd Division in this battle, its timeless epitaph reads: 'When you go home tell them of us and say / For your tomorrow, we gave our today.'

17 //// THE RETREAT FROM CHOSIN RESERVOIR, KOREA, 1950

*I*n late 1950, United Nations troops – consisting principally of United States personnel – defeated the offensive of the Korean People's Army, and threw the Communist North Koreans back beyond the 38th Parallel (the border that had partitioned the peninsula in 1945). Breaking out from the Pusan Perimeter in South Korea, the UN forces had temporarily defeated the North Koreans, using amphibious landings at the Battle of Inchon to crush what was left of their resistance. The UN advanced steadily northwards with the intention of eventually reuniting the two portions of the country. The People's Republic of China saw the situation very differently. Having struggled to win a civil war just a year before, China believed the Americans would attempt to roll back the Communist tide and invade China from its new Korean springboard. In secret, Chinese forces were amassed to strike back at the UN as they approached the Yalu River. The Chinese Ninth Army was redeployed from Manchuria so hastily that it was forced to leave behind its heavy artillery, but it was the failure to acquire any winter clothing that was to prove an even more costly oversight. On 15 October 1950, this People's Volunteer Army (PVA) slipped undetected across the Chinese border and into North Korea.

Facing them was the UN advance. On the western side of the Taebaek Mountains, which formed the spine of the country, lay the US Eighth Army, while to the east were the Republic of Korea 1 Corps and the US X Corps. In this eastern zone, a surprise attack was made by the Chinese 42nd Corps, which clashed with the South Koreans on 25 October in the Funchilin Pass, south of the Chosin Reservoir basin. Meanwhile, the 1st US Marine Division, which had landed on the east coast at Wonsan as part of the X Corps order of battle, engaged this forward Chinese element on 2 November. Taking heavy losses, the Chinese vanguard retreated towards the Chosin Reservoir itself. Within three weeks of this first contact, the Marines were in possession of the entire basin, with troops stationed at Sinhung-ni on the southern side of the reservoir and at Yudam-ni on the western side. To the west the Chinese had struck against the US Eighth Army, which was in difficulties. To relieve their pressure, General Douglas MacArthur, the UN commander in Korea, ordered X Corps to drive westwards and threaten the Chinese lines of communications. This, however, had the effect of stringing the corps out

Previous pages: **US Marines move forward in the Hagaru-ri area of Korea, after effective close-air support flushes out the enemy from their hillside entrenchment, December, 1950.**

across a long front, leaving it more vulnerable to a fresh Chinese offensive from the north.

The bulk of the PVA Ninth Army crossed the North Korean border on 10 November and arrived, undetected, around Chosin on 17 November. Chinese reconnaissance revealed a number of weaknesses in the UN dispositions. The two American garrisons on either side of the reservoir were unable to support each other, and it was clear that the road junction south of the reservoir at Hagaru-ri, – although strategically important – was only lightly defended. The Chinese were aware that the road running south of the reservoir to Koto-ri and on to the port of Hungnam appeared to be the Americans' only line of retreat. The Chinese plan was to neutralize the three positions around the reservoir and then, as the UN forces came in from the south to relieve them, they in turn would be encircled and destroyed. The only difficulty the Chinese had was determining the actual strength of the UN forces since time was short. They nevertheless felt confident that their 60,000 men could overwhelm the relatively small detachments confronting them. Moreover, by infiltrating and maximizing the element of surprise they would be able to defeat the Westerners while suffering relatively low casualties. What the Chinese commanders did not realize was that the US 1st Marine Division (reinforced by the British 41 Royal Marines Commando, and two American infantry battalions) had arrived at Yudam-ni, which meant that the total strength of UN forces was close to 27,000.

The Chinese began their attacks at night on 27 November. Ambushes were conducted against mobile units, while massive infantry assaults swept on to the defended garrisons around the reservoir. At Yudam-ni, the Marines were soon surrounded, and tried to make sense of the confused situation while fighting along a hastily formed perimeter. On the eastern side of the reservoir, Regiment Combat Team 31 found itself similarly isolated and under attack from two divisions, the 80th and 81st. Further south, US Marines at Koto-ri were being attacked by another division. Taken by surprise, each formation was initially fighting for its survival.

At Yudam-ni, the 5th US Marines tried to drive their assailants westwards and made attacks in the direction of Mupyong-ni, but they were soon pinned down by the Chinese 89th Division and subsequently attacked by five infantry battalions of the 79th, another Chinese division that had unexpectedly arrived in the vicinity. On the mountain slopes the Americans found the Chinese trying to infiltrate between their platoons, with only boulders and the folds in the ground for cover. Close-quarter fighting erupted both in front of and between the Americans' positions, and casualties were high on both sides. By dawn on the 28th, the five Chinese battalions had been so decimated they could take no further part in the battle.

Immediately to the south, the Chinese 59th Division encountered two companies of the 7th US Marines and subjected them to a ferocious attack. Only Charlie Company was able to extricate itself (and this with some difficulty) then fight its way back into the Yudam-ni pocket. Fox Company was not so fortunate and became cut off in the Toktong Pass. This defile was of great strategic value because it controlled the road between Yudam-ni and the junction at Hagaru-ri. The PVA 59th Division made repeated attempts to wipe out this Marine company, but the defenders clung to their rocks despite sub-zero temperatures, a lack of ammunition and rations, and the constant fire from the Chinese all around them. The US 7th Marines tried to break through to rescue the beleaguered force, but, despite inflicting grievous losses, they couldn't reach their comrades. For five days and nights, the Marines at Toktong held out alone and unsupported.

The Chinese commanders were surprised by the strength and tenacity of the Americans. They realized rather belatedly that there were far more Marines at Yudam-ni than they had initially estimated

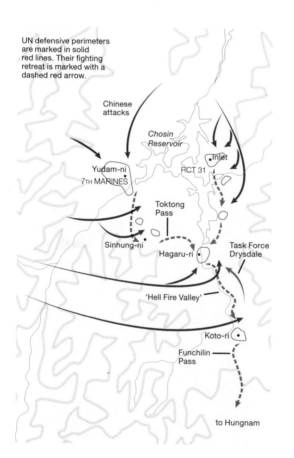

UN defensive perimeters are marked in solid red lines. Their fighting retreat is marked with a dashed red arrow.

At Chosin, UN forces had to break out of a closing ring of Chinese divisions. While some were cut off and had to be relieved, and others overrun and wiped out by vastly superior numbers, the remainder cut their way southwards and made a successful evacuation.

and they were concerned about the high casualties they had suffered already. The decision was therefore taken to switch the axis of their offensive in order to overrun the Hagaru-ri position, and then to cut off all the UN forces in the area. At the same time, the lull in attacks gave the surrounded Americans at Yudam-ni the chance to recover. It was at this point they received orders to make for Hungnam Port, orders that meant fighting their way out along a road 78 miles (126 km) long that was often overlooked by mountains, dissected by defiles and steep ridges, and made treacherous by ice and snow. For armoured support, the Marines had only one Sherman tank, although they could have air support when the weather permitted it. Even to begin, however, the 5th and 7th Marines realized that they would have to capture Hills 1419 and 1542, topography that dominated the route south, and furthermore they would have to make a fresh attempt to relieve Fox Company at the Toktong Pass.

The Chinese meanwhile launched the 79th, a fresh division, against the garrison of Yudam-ni on 1 December. Using the cover of darkness, the Chinese infantry bravely advanced into a storm of small-arms fire and made such progress that the Marines' rearguard was forced to call in airstrikes to break up the Chinese formations. Vast explosions lit up the night and the Americans slipped away from Yudam-ni. At the head of the Marines' column, the attack on Hill 1419 was already underway. Artillery and air bombardments devastated the defenders, and the PVA 59th Division that held the hill was forced to commit the last company from its reserve. The survivors, a mixture of units, refused to relinquish the high ground and it was not until nightfall on 1 December that the Marines finally managed to secure the heights. The Chinese they found lacked rations and winter equipment, and it was evident that many had suffered from frostbite. For the Marines, taking the hill represented a tactical victory of some significance. Dominating the surrounding landscape, they were able to advance on either side of the road leading south, and in doing so, surprise or encircle Chinese blocking positions. On 2 December, the 7th Marines were able to launch an attack towards the Toktong Pass, while, simultaneously, Fox Company made a breakout assault. The pass was soon in American hands, freeing up another stage of the route south.

The Americans still had to fight their way at every step of the retreat. Individual Chinese posts opened up on the column of vehicles at every opportunity, causing significant delays. On 2 December, the Chinese launched a major night attack with their infantry, sweeping out of the hills and causing heavy losses among the Marines. The assault was beaten off only after a prolonged firefight and the arrival of American jets, which blasted the Chinese positions.

While the Yudam-ni garrison managed to extricate itself, the Regimental Combat Team 31 (RCT 31) had been less fortunate. This reduced brigade was stretched across a large area at the start of the battle and on the night of 27 November a Chinese division had sought to wipe them out. Many individual units were overrun and completely destroyed and by the end of the night, RCT 31 found itself in three isolated pockets: surrounded, outnumbered and overlooked by the Chinese on Hill 1221. As fortune would have it, many Chinese troops believed that the battle was over at dawn, and they began to loot the stores they found in the RCT perimeter for the clothing and food that they so desperately needed. This lack of battle discipline gave the Americans an opportunity to counter-attack, and the 3rd Battalion, 31st Infantry, although severely outgunned, assaulted the main Chinese force at a position known as the Inlet. The sudden attack took the Chinese by surprise and the PVA troops fell back hastily during the confusion. The Americans considered a more deliberate pursuit, but fresh Chinese attacks soon dispelled such optimism on that score. Three Chinese regiments from the 80th Division made a night attack, but the configuration of the ground at the Inlet and problems in communication caused the attack to lose cohesion. As the leading Chinese infantry came within range of the Americans, the US 57th Field Artillery Battalion used its 40 mm anti-aircraft guns in an anti-person-nel role. The heavy rounds tore through the densely packed Chinese ranks and some shells struck the rocky terrain, adding to the shrapnel effect and increasing the number of casualties. Both advancing and retreating Chinese units were cut to pieces by this gunfire. Only 600 of the division's men survived, but the PVA commanders were still eager to resume the offensive and deployed wings to work their way around the Americans' flanks.

The Americans knew it was only a matter of time before another assault was launched and they fully anticipated heavy artillery bombardments by the Chinese. Consequently, 31st Tank Company tried to open up a route to RCT 31 by storming Hill 1221. Without integral infantry units, however, the unsupported armour strug-gled to scale the steep terrain or to defeat infantry. The attacks, occurring over two successive days, failed. Within the RCT 31 perimeter, ammunition was running low along with other combat supplies. There were also a number of wounded men to evacuate, and that meant fresh attempts would have to be made to take Hill 1221.

//

162

The Chinese were determined to destroy RCT 31 before it could slip away and replaced their existing formations with the 94th Division before a major night attack was launched on 30 November. Despite the fighting continuing well into the next day, the Americans' again clung to their positions. RCT 31 planned to attempt a breakout, but even before the column of vehicles had formed, another PVA assault was made. The perimeter was now in danger of complete collapse and it was clear that only the most desperate measures could save the unit from being destroyed. Air support was an option, but the Chinese had already engaged in a close-quarter battle with the Americans. The extreme decision was taken to order a napalm drop right on the vanguard of their own column, despite the losses this would obviously entail. The effect was utterly devastating. The slopes that lay in front of the Americans erupted in vast orange balls of fire and oily black smoke. Chinese infantry still working their way forward were incinerated.

Although the momentum of the Chinese attack was reduced, it was only a temporary respite for the men of RCT 31. As they attempted to push forward, the Chinese troops left alive in the rocks and ravines of Hill 1221 opened fire and pinned down the assaulting troops. Any soldiers scrambling up the slopes were swiftly cut down. As the vehicles of the column inched their way along the road that ran below the summit they were raked with gunfire. Wounded men were hit again, drivers were killed and there was the risk that these survivors would be overtaken by the three Chinese Regiments that were now converging on them from the north. Lieutenant Colonel Don Carlos Faith Jr (the commander of RCT 31) inspired his men whenever he went among them, keeping the troops moving and fighting as best he could. When the column was halted by a Chinese roadblock he led the platoon attack personally, but was wounded mortally when a grenade exploded. It took a gargantuan effort to assault and eventually clear the roadblock. The column continued through the hills, still subjected to machine-gun fire at every step until they were once more halted by a Chinese roadblock. This time, the Chinese started to pour fire down from every side. Hundreds of PVA started to skirmish forward, the RCT 31 defenders taking what cover they could among the boulders and trucks. Fighting was now at close quarters, and the Americans were being wiped out, a handful at a time. Small groups tried to fight their way out of the trap, some successfully, others not. Only 385 survived unscathed to reach Hagaru-ri.

The small garrison at Hagaru-ri had been fighting just as desperately from the beginning of the Chinese offensive. Storemen, cooks and drivers had been pressed into the firing line to augment the inadequate number of riflemen available. It was still not enough. In a daring night attack, the Chinese had managed to penetrate the perimeter, cut down some of the defenders, and charge into the logistics areas. Once there, however, their cohesion and direction collapsed, giving the Americans time to launch hasty counter-attacks that gradually drove the Chinese troops out. At dawn, the Chinese remained in possession of the East Hill on the base's northern perimeter, but had been driven back and surrendered all their other gains.

To assist the embattled garrison of Hagaru-ri, a relief detachment was despatched from Koto-ri further south on 29 November. The group was nicknamed Task Force Drysdale after its commander, a British officer who led both the unit and the spearhead element of 41 Commando Royal Marines. G Company, 1st Marines and B Company, 31st Infantry completed the relief force. This tiny composite battalion faced a near-impossible task, and came under constant attack from the PVA 60th Division from the start. The road that marked the axis of the advance was soon dubbed 'Hell Fire Valley' because of the intensity of the bombardments zeroing-in there. During the day, one disabled vehicle blocked the progress of the force and attacks by the Chinese broke the formation into two parts. The lead element pressed on and managed to reach Hagaru-ri after dark. The rear element was completely wiped out by Chinese attacks.

At Hagaru-ri the next day, fresh attempts were made to retake East Hill, but it remained in Chinese hands with high numbers of casualties on both sides. On 30 November, the remaining troops of the Chinese 58th Division assembled for a final overnight assault on the perimeter of Hagaru-ri, using the East Hill as part of their assembly area. Initially they enjoyed some success and the UN defences around the base of East Hill were overrun, but as the 58th tried to get further forward they were cut down. Machine-gun fire and the guns of the 31st Tank Company forced the Chinese to fall back, and rendered them unable to mount further offensive operations.

A few days after the epic defence of these UN perimeters, the breakout from the reservoir could begin in earnest. When the 5th Marines arrived at Hagaru-ri, they were able to assist in the retaking of the East Hill and help secure the UN lines. In the interval, Chinese reinforcements had also arrived but the chance to snuff out the defenders at Hagaru-ri had passed. When two fresh PVA divisions made a night attack, they were thrown back and destroyed without taking a single objective. The US 7th Marines had meanwhile taken the high ground on either side of the road to the south. The Chinese therefore shifted their attacks to these heights in the hope of cutting off the retreat. Again, Chinese assaults were delivered with great determination and at the cost of heavy casualties. The UN column was reduced to a snail's pace as each attack was beaten off, while American aircraft were busy strafing Chinese attackers as they tried to form up. By 7 December, the UN forces had made it to Koto-ri – safe, if tired and battle-worn by their experiences.

The Chinese now renewed their efforts to pursue the Americans and positioned the remnants of their 20th Corps, which had borne the brunt of earlier fighting, on the UN withdrawal route. Attempts were made by the Chinese to blow the Treadway Bridge near the Funchilin Pass and they rendered it impassable. The 1st US Marines subsequently took the adjacent high ground known as Hill 1081 in a sharp action, and a new bridge was constructed. The Marines were astonished to find that, while the Chinese at Hill 1081 had fought to the last man, some troops had frozen to death in their dugouts and fox holes. The critical supply situation in the Chinese PVA had reached the point of crisis, and their men were dying of starvation or hypothermia. Although the Chinese could still muster more men and make attacks on the UN rearguard, the Americans had the firepower to defeat them.

The UN forces finally reached Hungnam on 11 December having fought continuously for 15 days. While an evacuation was organized, the US Navy provided additional fire support to the garrison, which helped repulse the final offensives of the depleted PVA Ninth Army. It took less than two weeks to extract the entire force from Hungnam. Despite all the odds against them, the UN had carried out a fighting retreat and managed to bring away over 100,000 troops, a similar number of Korean civilians, 17,500 vehicles and 350,000 tons of combat supplies. The PVA had been deprived of its showpiece victory and its Ninth Army had ceased to exist as a combat effective force (until substantially reconstituted the following year). While casualty figures were never agreed, even official Chinese sources admitted to losses in excess of 50,000 men. The UN lost 1,029 killed, with a further 4,852 wounded and 5,000 missing. The figures show that the UN had been able to withdraw under constant pressure and still operate as an effective force, inflicting grievous losses on an enemy that was not only substantially larger, but also possessed the initiative at the start of the operations.

18 //// THE DEFENCE OF THE GOLAN HEIGHTS, ISRAEL, 1973

Stung by a crippling defeat in 1967 during the Six Day War, the Arab states of Egypt and Syria were eager to take their revenge against Israel and wipe it from the map. Steady progress had been made with the rearmament of their armies thanks to Soviet Union and Eastern Bloc support, but Israel enjoyed the backing of the United States and obtained its military hardware from the Western nations. The Middle East was engaged in an arms race, fully aware that a conflict would erupt at some stage. Throughout 1973 Cairo radio was full of anti-Israeli rhetoric, and there were other signs that the Egyptians were preparing for a confrontation. Israel's Prime Minister, Golda Meir, was not enthusiastic about launching another 1967-style surprise offensive as a pre-emptive strike. Her Defence Minister (and hero of the Six Day War), Moshe Dayan, also advised caution. The alignment of world superpowers behind the Arab and Israeli adversaries had the potential to earn the opprobrium of the international community, or even precipitate a major war. Yet Egypt, Syria and their Arab allies continued preparations. Their plan was to launch a surprise attack, with Egypt heading east across the Suez Canal and seizing the western Sinai, while Syria attacked Israel from the north to overrun the defences on the Golan Heights. To add to their advantage, the Arab states would strike during the Jewish holiday of Yom Kippur.

The Golan Heights dominate the entire border of Israel and Syria, and command of these uplands not only controls northern Israel but also offers a straight avenue to Damascus, giving the area strategic importance to both countries. Stretching for 24 miles (40 km) to the east of the River Jordan, the hills were dissected by five key roads running east–west, as well as two routes that traversed north to south. The Syrians deployed five divisions to carry out their planned offensive: the 7th Infantry Division was to advance parallel to Mount Hermon, the highest point on the hills, while to their immediate south, the 9th Infantry Division would push into the Israeli centre. The main attack would be delivered by the 5th Infantry Division in the area known as the Rafid Gap, pressing west and southwest towards the River Jordan. The 3rd Armoured Division and the 1st Armoured Division would lead the assault, and also support the infantry. In addition, waves of aircraft would strafe Israeli positions, knock out their tanks and interdict their reinforcements. The Syrians could muster 1,000 artillery pieces and 1,500 tanks to

Previous pages: **Israeli tanks on the Golan Heights, Yom Kippur War, 1973.**

lay down suppressive fire. Many of these vehicles were the latest Soviet models, such as the T-62 with a 115 mm main armament. The Russians were particularly eager to see how their new equipment performed in these favourable conditions. The Syrians believed it would take them just 36 hours to overrun the entire area.

The Israelis were seriously outnumbered. On the Golan Heights, there was a network of 17 small concrete observation posts manned with garrisons of up to platoon strength, some possessing a troop of three or four tanks. Initially there had been only 50 tanks along the whole front, but the prospect of war meant that reinforcements had been mobilized, bringing the total to 150. This was still a meagre force to face 1,500 armoured vehicles. Fortunately, the Israelis had the rugged and battle-tested American M60 and British Centurion to confront the Soviet-built armour. There were, however, just 60 guns distributed along the 45 mile (70 km) line, and the only personnel for the defence of this strategically important zone were the 7th and 188th armoured brigades.

The Syrian offensive began at 1400 hours on Saturday 6 October with an overwhelming artillery barrage and air attack that lasted almost an hour. Shell after shell plummeted onto the Israeli strongpoints, detonating with an earsplitting crash, the explosions tearing up the soil and vegetation. Syrian tank commanders watching the debris and columns of smoke could hear the crump of explosions above the roar of their engines, and they started towards their objectives under cover of the bombardment. Meanwhile, Syrian commandos landed by helicopter around the summit of Mount Hermon and dashed up to the gates of the radar station located on the vantage point. The gates of the outpost were defended by only 14 Israelis, so the Syrian special forces battalion was able to work its way forward under cover of machine-gun fire, overrun the incomplete trench system and fight their way into the bunkers. The tiny garrison was soon wiped out.

As Hermon was being captured, the lead elements of Syria's 3rd Armoured Division and the 7th Infantry Division engaged the Israeli 7th Brigade to the north of the battlefield, and the main Syrian thrust got underway at the Rafid Gap. Here the Israeli 188th Brigade, with its 57 tanks, faced 600 Syrian vehicles. Every few minutes, Syrian or Israeli armour would be hit and explode, while the other tank crews tried desperately to manoeuvre into the best-protected firing points with the largest fields of fire. They worked their guns feverishly, conscious that survival depended on spotting the enemy and engaging him successfully before they were themselves hit and blown to oblivion. The sheer violence of the fighting reflected the intensity of modern armoured warfare: rounds slammed into hulls and turrets, tearing vehicles apart; flames burst from stricken tanks; and black, oily smoke poured across the battlefield. Amid the inferno, survivors who had managed to bail out staggered or crawled into whatever cover they could find.

Only a handful of Israeli tanks survived the initial onslaught. Some, already damaged and carrying the bodies of their comrades, had taken shelter to the west of the Tapline Road. There they met Lieutenant Zwicka Gringold, a young officer who had rushed back from leave to join the battle. Gringold cleared the bodies from the decks of the tanks and formed a small composite force of survivors that could take the fight back to the Syrians. 'Force Zwicka', as they styled themselves, consisted of just four tanks. As they drove back up the road, every man in that valiant command must have been fully aware of the odds against him. They all knew that their chances of survival were practically zero.

The Syrian 1st Armoured Division was, by contrast, confident of victory. The attack had been developing well all afternoon, and Israeli positions were being steadily overwhelmed and neutralized. Little now stood between them and the Israeli Divisional Headquarters at Nafekh and, beyond that, the Bnot Ya'akov Bridge over the Jordan. It was clear that the Syrians were advancing all along the line, and that it was only a matter of time before they rolled down into the plains to the west.

Gringold had positioned his four tanks to engage the head of the Syrian 1st Armoured Division. As night began to fall, the Syrian tanks were hit again and again. Then, with a boldness verging on suicidal recklessness, Gringold's tanks drove into the midst of the Syrian units under cover of the failing light. Since Syrian tanks were often not equipped with radios, there was little chance for them to coordinate a coherent defence. The result was chaotic – the Israeli tanks destroying the Syrians around them and causing utter confusion. As the Syrians tried to re-establish some formation, Gringold's men would fire from a flank, move into another position and fire again. The Syrians weren't sure exactly what size force they were dealing with, and for 20 hours Force Zwicka kept up its game of cat and mouse. The battlefield was now littered with damaged and burning vehicles. Some of Gringold's men were forced to abandon their own tanks and find others to continue the fight. Eventually, Force Zwicka was reduced to just one serviceable vehicle, but still the survivors would not give up. The security of northern Israel depended on them.

By first light on the following day, Sunday 7 October, the Syrian 1st Armoured Division was ready to continue its advance. Israel's 188th Brigade was all but wiped out. The last few tanks, directed in person by the Brigade's commander, Colonel Ben-Shoham, stood their ground on the Tapline Road, fighting to the death. Over 90 per cent of the brigade officers were killed or wounded during those 24 hours, sacrificing themselves to buy time for their comrades behind. They were determined to take as many Syrians with them as possible.

The Israelis knew that time was of the essence. Men and tanks arriving from their mobilization points drove straight into battle. Units arrived piecemeal, but the objective was simply to stem the Syrian tide and resist with whatever they had. There was no sophisticated plan, no scheme of manoeuvre: it was a case of fight or die. The Syrians nevertheless kept rolling on towards Nafekh Headquarters. Then, at this critical point, Gringold and his exhausted band in their single tank suddenly burst out of the hills and destroyed the leading Syrian T-62. With high explosive rounds chasing them, they slipped back over a ridge.

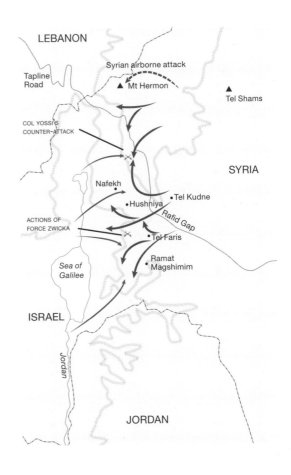

On the Golan Heights, at the height of the surprise Yom Kippur War, pockets of Israeli forces were able to survive the initial Syrian armoured offensives. These held the line and provided the spearhead for a more sustained counter-attack that pushed the Syrians back into their own territory.

As the Syrians sent their tanks into the Nafekh encampment, more Israelis joined the defiant resistance. By mid-afternoon, the Syrian attack was stalling, halted about halfway through the complex. The Syrians attempted an outflanking drive to the south at the village of Ramat Magshimim, but this was also blocked. In the south, the Israeli line was holding.

Further north, the Israeli 7th Brigade with a total of 100 tanks was confronted by over 500 Syrian armoured vehicles. For four days and nights the engagement was unceasing. Both sides launched several assaults each day and at least two by night in an attempt to secure the ground. Eventually the sheer weight of numbers decided the outcome. With just seven tanks left intact, the Israelis simply could not prevent the Syrians getting forward at every point and began to pull back. As they did so, they met Lieutenant Colonel Yossi Ben-Hanan with a column of 13 hastily repaired tanks coming up the road. Among the crews were wounded men who had volunteered to rejoin the fight. Bandaged, but defiant, these extraordinary men manoeuvred alongside the seven remaining vehicles of 7th Brigade while the plan for a sudden counter-attack was worked out.

The Syrians, who believed the Israelis to be beaten, were surprised by Yossi's fierce counterstroke. Thinking the battle was over, the tired and battered Syrian crews were demoralized by this fresh wave of Israeli attacks. Having already lost 500 tanks, a full third of their original strength, and casting an eye over the 'Valley of Tears' (as they called the battlefield), the Syrians decided they had had enough. Several Israeli strongpoints, which had held out throughout the four-day battle, reported that the Syrian support vehicles had turned around and were withdrawing – a sure sign the lead elements were also soon to pull back. Then surely the most extraordinary scene in modern armoured warfare was played out – the mass of Syrian vehicles retreated, pursued to the border area by a handful of Israeli tanks.

Soon after, Israel mobilization produced an armoured division under the command of Major General Moshe 'Musa' Peled for a counter-attack in the southern sector, where the Syrian forces had not retreated. The fighting was just as fierce as before, but Peled's new formation began to drive back the invading forces. The Syrians tried to stem the Israeli advance by bringing up the full force of the Syrian 1st Armoured Division. The leading Israeli brigade found itself in a salient between Syrian armoured formations and under attack from several sides. The

Syrians, however, were also in a precarious position. Having committed a large portion of their armour and infantry to capture Hushniya, in the centre of the Golan Heights, there was a risk that the success of Israeli counter-attacks on either side could leave the Syrians encircled in a pocket. To make matters worse, the Israeli air force (now restored after initial attacks), had destroyed a number of Syrian aircraft and neutralized several surface-to-air missile batteries. The Israeli pilots now began to turn their attention to Syrian ground forces. To break out of the potential encirclement, the Syrians changed the axis of their attacks towards Peled's command in the south. Peled was undeterred and made the boldest of decisions: he ordered his leading elements to thrust further eastwards as far as possible into the Syrian depth. The move helped the Israelis gain possession of Tel Faris, a peak that would prove an ideal observation platform for artillery.

The Syrians used the cover of darkness to pull back, regroup and send a force to cut across the Israeli advance. The following morning – the fourth day of the fighting – Peled tried to get forward to Tel Kudne, where the Syrian divisional headquarters were located; however, the action cost him many tanks. The Israelis had more success in reducing the resistance of the Syrians around Hushniya, where not one Syrian tank remained in action at the end of the day. Chaim Herzog (who took part in the conflict, and went on to become a military historian and the Prime Minister of Israel) described the scene in the pocket as 'one large graveyard of Syrian vehicles and equipment. Hundreds of guns, supply vehicles, APCs, fuel vehicles, BRDM Sagger armoured missile carriers, tanks and tons of ammunition were dotted around the hills and slopes surrounding Hushniya.' Still outnumbered, the Israelis now drove the Syrians back to their initial lines, providing an unlikely outcome to one of the greatest tank battles of history.

The war was not yet over – the Israeli forces were exceedingly vulnerable. Teams worked furiously to patch up damaged vehicles and get them back into action. Columns of supplies and ammunition had to be driven to the frontline units. Men had to be deployed into the threatened points. Within just two days, the Israelis were not just ready to defend against any further Syrian thrusts, but they were prepared to take the war to the enemy. General Ben-Gal, the overall commander, addressed his officers prior to the counter-offensive. Many were tired and struggling to stay awake, but his speech was particularly moving and uplifting. The men were inspired for one last effort. Two wings were organized and, crossing the international frontier, the Israelis drove into depleted Syrian formations (supported by their Moroccan and Iraqi allies).

The Israelis, including the refitted and reinforced 188th Brigade, managed to burst through the Syrian minefields and defeat the armour and anti-tank crews waiting for them. The 7th Brigade engaged in similarly bitter fighting, and, after a six-hour battle, took key road junctions and villages at strategic points. Colonel Yossi was also back in action. He had to attack the hill feature known as Tel Shams on three occasions, but each time was forced back by the Sagger anti-tank missiles that hurtled towards his vehicles. Large boulders made it difficult to manoeuvre, and an attempt by Israeli infantry to cross the open ground also failed. After further reconnaissance, Yossi found a hidden route through the boulder fields, and led eight tanks to the rear of the summit where he engaged the Syrians with a surprise attack. Anti-tank missiles smashed into each of his vehicles, and Yossi himself was thrown from the turret of the lead tank. At nightfall, this wounded officer was rescued by a paratroop unit that stormed the hill. They succeeded in capturing this key position having lost only four men wounded.

The Israelis continued to press on with their advance towards Damascus, and the Syrians were forced to pull every available unit into the area. The Syrians, desperate to save their capital, massed huge concentrations of artillery and equipped infantry with anti-tank weapons, ordering them to take up positions ahead of the main defence lines under cover of darkness. President Assad called the Egyptians and pleaded with them to intensify their offensive in the Sinai to save Syria. It was a fateful request. As the Egyptians advanced beyond their anti-aircraft missile screen, deeper into the Sinai, the Israelis had the opportunity to use their skill in combined arms operations to defeat the Egyptian offensive. So successful was their counter-attack that, within days, the Israelis had managed to reach the Suez Canal and cross it, threatening the rear of the leading Egyptian divisions.

The Israelis managed to wrest back all of their lost ground on the Golan Heights and recaptured Mount Hermon on 22 October. That evening, Syria accepted a ceasefire proposed by the United Nations. They had lost 1,150 tanks, and their Iraqi and Jordanian allies had lost a further 150. Some 3,500 Syrians had been killed and 370 taken prisoner. The Israelis had lost 250 tanks, but 150 of them had been repaired and put back into action. Almost all the tanks had been hit at some point during the fighting but were still categorized as battle-worthy. The Israelis had lost 772 men, and 2,453 were wounded (although many of the latter had managed to fight on throughout the battle). All ranks had exhibited the most extraordinary courage and determination to overcome the odds against them. The battle for the Golan Heights in 1973 therefore must surely rank among the most outstanding feats of human endeavour in modern warfare.

19 /// THE BATTLE OF DEBECKA, IRAQ, 2003

*T*he American strategy for the invasion of Iraq was designed to make the best use of new technologies and assets to utilize their speed and firepower in order to create a deep psychological impact on the forces of Saddam Hussein. In contrast to the Gulf War of 1990–91, there would be no long preparatory air campaign prior to a ground assault. Instead there would be a simultaneous and combined land–air invasion that would emphasize the effects of the forces' superiority in weaponry and their ability to manoeuvre. The approach was summed up in the expression 'shock and awe', and it was hoped that these tactics would break the enemy's will to fight.

In the weeks preceding the attack, the Turkish government refused to allow the Western-led coalition to use their border as a springboard against Iraq. This refusal was partly a response to the American plan to use Kurdish irregulars, the Peshmerga, to augment their ground forces. The Turkish government had been plagued with Kurdish attacks for decades and had no wish to cooperate with these old adversaries. Consequently, the American invasion plan had to be modified. Instead of heavy armour arriving from the north and south in a two-pronged thrust, the main attack would come from the south, with amphibious operations along the coast. In the north, lightly equipped special forces would be deployed with close air support. Such light forces would be even more reliant on speed for their survival, and units were provided with all-terrain vehicles (ATVs) known to the troops as 'War Pigs' or GMVs (the latter being converted Humvees). In fact, in the campaign that followed, the troops were often dependent on converted civilian vehicles – such as Land Rovers and Toyotas – tooled up with an array of weapons and communications equipment. Luckily, the troops were used to improvisation.

The 10th Special Forces Group (Airborne) and the 3rd Battalion 3rd Special Forces Group (which had just returned from Afghanistan) consisted of highly mobile Operational Detachment Alpha (ODA) teams who could call on various supporting assets, including resupply vehicle groups known as Advanced Operating Bases. Elements of the 173rd Airborne Brigade and 10th Mountain Division were attached and airpower was in the hands of the 123rd Special Tactics Squadron. Together the formation was known as Task Force Viking, a suitably warlike sobriquet. Only the 10th had the advantage of having operated in the area before, during

Previous pages: **US invasion troops in Iraq, March, 2003.**

the humanitarian relief mission known as Operation Provide Comfort (1991–96), so gathering information was in part dependent on local allies. The mission now was to prevent 13 Iraqi infantry and armoured divisions from reinforcing Baghdad as the main coalition thrust worked its way up from the south. While the skills and courage of the special forces teams were not in doubt, no one could predict how this new doctrine of pitting light forces against conventional divisions would turn out. In fact, it would be tested to the limit in the battle for the Debecka crossroads.

In February 2003, the special forces teams touched down at Arbil in northern Iraq thanks to the arrangements of CIA agents who had been deployed covertly the previous year. Although the landings were opposed by Iraqi anti-aircraft fire, a total of 51 ODAs were landed and they soon linked up with over 60,000 Peshmerga fighters drawn from the Patriotic Union of Kurdistan. Parachute landings were also made to secure oilfields near Kirkuk.

The first mission of the special forces was not, in fact, to neutralize Iraqi conventional forces, but to raid and suppress the headquarters of the Ansar al-Islam, an organization led by, among others, the notorious Abu Musa al-Zarqawi (the individual who later went on to command the militant group al-Qaeda in Iraq and commit acts of wholesale murder and terror against Iraqis). The headquarters were located in a valley defended by over 1,000 insurgents and militant Kurdish fighters who opposed the Peshmerga. To soften up their defences, Tomahawk cruise missile strikes were first called in. Advancing into the Sargat Valley along several lines of attack, the ODAs and their Peshmerga allies were repeatedly held up by heavy machine-gun fire from bunkers and entrenched positions. The defenders were carefully winkled out with precision airstrikes, and fire from grenade launchers or the .50 calibre machine guns mounted on the special forces' ATVs. The village of Sargat was taken, but stiffer resistance was encountered at Daramar Gorge. Here caves provided the Ansar fighters with plenty of cover from air attack, though the ODAs and Peshmerga were able to suppress the insurgent groups sufficiently to make a clean break. While some of the Ansar chose this moment to make good their escape to Iran, a few chose to fight it out to the end. Once the ODAs had gained the high ground, these remaining pockets were mopped up relatively easily. There were no American casualties, and in total the Ansar lost 300 men. Interestingly, scientific teams later discovered IED (Improvised Explosive Device) 'factories' as well as evidence of experimentation with ricin, a deadly poison. Whether these were being developed by the Ansar or left over from the Iran–Iraq War of the 1980s is not clear.

Task Force Viking now pressed on towards Ayn Sifni, a town on the highway to Mosul. Control of this route would prevent any Iraqi counter-offensive against the strategically important cities and oilfields of the north. Air power again proved decisive, and it seemed that the Iraqi defences were broken up. Intelligence esti-mates calculated that only two platoons (some 60 men) remained; however, the leading ODA was met with a storm of gunfire. It soon became apparent that the Iraqis were still entrenched in battalion strength, with mortars, armour, anti-aircraft guns and artillery. For four hours, three ODAs and 300 Peshmerga engaged the Iraqi battalion using 'fast air' – ground attack aircraft armed with a variety of bombs and missiles – to hammer the Iraqis. After this tremendous bombardment the ODAs were able to get into Ayn Sifni, but almost immediately they were sub-jected to an Iraqi light infantry counter-attack, and salvos of mortar fire. Once again, the ODAs engaged with what light armaments they possessed and brought down precision airstrikes. The Iraqi attackers melted away.

To the southeast, an even more epic action was developing at the Debecka junction. The crossroads near the village was the key to the north, as it was the point where the highways to Mosul and Kirkuk met. The Iraqis clearly understood its significance and troops (some dug in) were located around the site and on the Zurqah Ziraw Dagh Ridge that overlooked it.

Prior to the advance of the ODAs, B-52 bombers saturated the target with heavy ordnance. This achieved, ODA 044 with 150 Peshmerga drove towards Objective Rock, a junction just short of the main crossroads by the town of Debecka. ODAs 391 and 392 provided this force with fire support. To the north, 500 Peshmerga (split into two units) were tasked with the capture of the ridge. Further north still, three ODAs and 150 Peshmerga set out to take Objective Stone, a hilltop occupied by Iraqis on the flank of the coalition forces' advance.

The Peshmerga on the ridge seized their objective against token resistance, but the battle for Objective Stone was more confused. Airstrikes had failed either to hit the targets or suppress the defenders. Two ODAs engaged, but were subjected to a withering fire from heavy machine guns and mortars. Under these circum-stances, the accompanying Peshmerga refused to go forward. Calling for more air support, the two ODAs managed to extract, resupply and rejoin the fight. The

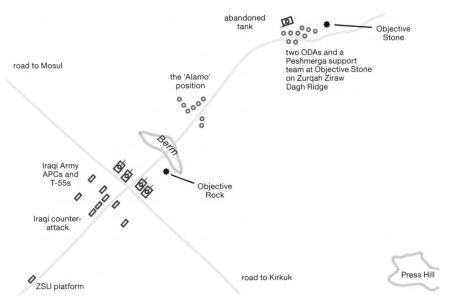

abandoned
tank

Objective
Stone

two ODAs and a
Peshmerga support
team at Objective Stone
on Zurqah Ziraw
Dagh Ridge

road to Mosul

the 'Alamo'
position

Berm

Iraqi Army
APCs and
T-55s

Objective
Rock

Iraqi counter-
attack

road to Kirkuk

Press Hill

ZSU platform

On the advance from northern Iraq towards Baghdad, American special forces teams and their
Kurdish irregular allies came under attack at the Debecka crossroads from more numerous
and better-armed Iraqi regular armoured forces. With nowhere to run, and facing imminent
destruction, the Americans fought it out resolutely.

remaining ODA, 043, had nevertheless managed to restart the attack themselves
and together with the Peshmerga they routed the battered Iraqi defenders. Objective
Stone had been captured.

As three ODAs, 044, 391 and 392, approached Objective Rock, they were
confronted by a dirt berm thrown across the road, liberally scattered with mines
and IEDs. The Peshmerga stopped to dismantle the obstacle, while the ODAs
attempted to bypass it. As they crested a low ridge, they came under the effective
fire (that is, with rounds falling among them) of Iraqi infantry dug in and occupying bunkers just beyond it. Too close to call in airstrikes, the ODAs simply let loose
with everything they had. It didn't take long for the Iraqi infantry to capitulate.

The Iraqi commanding officer then disclosed to the ODA that his armoured
support, which had until recently been with him, had driven away to the south.
Expecting a counter-attack, the teams drove back to the dirt berm barrier to effect
a breach should they later need to make a rapid withdrawal. From there, they then
sped on up to another ridge, known later as Press Hill, to carry out a covert

observation of the route south. Seemingly clear of enemy armour, the ODAs then pushed on to the crossroads.

On the approach to the crossroads, an Iraqi mortar platoon was sighted as it withdrew to Debecka. ODA 392 set off in pursuit, but were halted by the fire of a ZSU-57-2: an armoured anti-aircraft tracked vehicle with two heavy machine guns. This fire continued to play on the ODA teams during the events that followed. ODA 391 had more luck, destroying lightly armoured vehicles with its Javelin (anti-tank guided missiles) and the .50 calibre machine gun on board.

It was at this point that the special forces teams noticed a number of Iraqi APCs coming on from the crossroads, pouring smoke from generators to create a screen for some hidden formation behind. The ODAs engaged with .50 calibres and tried to ready the Javelins, but the Command Launch Units (trigger mechanisms) take a few moments to warm up, and in those few seconds, several Iraqi T-55 tanks emerged from the smoke, firing their main 100 mm tank guns at the ODA vehicles. The special forces teams were not equipped to take on this sort of heavy armour, and the only sensible thing to do was to temporarily pull back and try to bring in air support. Their escape rendezvous point was nicknamed 'the Alamo', and was designated as a place for a last-ditch stand some 985 yards (900 metres) from the crossroads. The trouble was, as they sped back under Iraqi tank fire, that no air support would be available for 30 minutes. The troops were aware that by then they could all be dead, so they had no choice but to try and fight it out as best they could.

The Iraqi APCs and tanks were gradually closing on the ODAs, and the special forces men all but exhausted their supply of Javelins, launching missile after missile at the line of approaching targets. Several Iraqi vehicles were hit and destroyed, and their attack stalled. Regrouping, the Iraqi tanks changed direction, advancing obliquely using folds in the ground to conceal themselves from the Javelin barrage. Iraqi small-arms fire continued to pour into the Alamo position – so much so that it seemed time had run out for the special forces group.

Just at that moment a flight of two US Navy F14s screeched overhead, and the special forces teams tried to talk the pilots onto the first T-55. Mistaking a rusty tank hulk nearby as the target, one F14 dropped a 2,000 lb bomb, not on the Iraqis, but on the Peshmerga and the ODA support team at Objective Stone. The BBC correspondent John Simpson, who was with the unit, described vividly the effect of this error live to viewers just moments after the detonation: 'This is just a scene from hell here. All the vehicles are on fire. There are bodies burning around me.' Twelve Peshmerga and four ODA were killed, while one cameraman was wounded. ODA 391 pulled back to give assistance, as the other ODA teams tried to offer them covering fire and extract from the Alamo to Press Hill.

Now the ODA teams found themselves under more intense Iraqi artillery fire, and the Iraqi tanks lurking nearby tried to get a fix on their position. One T-55 lurched forward, trying to get a clear shot with its main gun, but it was blasted with a Javelin and exploded. As the Iraqi shells began to land closer in, American F/A-18 jets arrived and hunted off the remaining Iraqi tanks. The special forces team had pulled through. A day later, American Task Force 1-63 arrived with M1A1 tanks and Bradley Fighting Vehicles, so there was no chance of any successful Iraqi counter-attack.

The results of the Battle of Debecka were impressive. Miraculously, the 26 special forces men had survived unscathed, holding off a reinforced Iraqi armoured battalion – with its tanks, artillery and mortar teams – long enough for air support to arrive. The Iraqis had made a conventional attack, but, despite their strength, they had failed to overrun the relatively small and lightly armed force. Admittedly American air power was critical, but for over half an hour during the battle, this asset was simply not available and the special forces had survived the onslaught against the odds. Moreover, their Peshmerga allies had been dispersed among other positions, carrying out separate tasks during the mission. In any case, these Kurdish irregulars had no anti-tank weapons to stop the Iraqi armour. The special forces teams had relied on their own integral weapons, robust communications and a great deal of courage to take on such a large formation. Each ODA team had sought the best position to continue the engagement, and, professional to the last, there was no question of abandoning the mission.

Special forces and reconnaissance troops are useful but they are always vulnerable: the operation had underscored the importance of having heavy weapon support close by during any light or airborne operations. It is evident that special forces need to be able to improvise, and to have enough firepower to stave off defeat if it all goes wrong, meaning there often has to be a trade-off between mobility and capability. Yet, above all, it is the human qualities that matter.

20 /// THE DEFENCE OF THE PLATOON HOUSES AND THE BATTLE OF WANAT, AFGHANISTAN, 2006–8

O n 11 September 2001 the movement known as al-Qaeda made its most audacious and murderous attack against the West. Hijacking four airliners, they attempted to destroy symbols of American power: two of the planes were flown like airborne bombs into the twin towers of the World Trade Center, another hit the Pentagon and a fourth, probably destined for the White House in Washington, DC, crashed in Pennsylvania when the passengers fought back and stormed the cockpit. Nearly 3,000 died in the world's worst terrorist attack and the United States – backed by a world-wide coalition – sought to hunt down al-Qaeda, to deny them training facilities, finances and freedom of movement. It was evident that the militant Islamist Taliban regime of Afghanistan had hosted al-Qaeda, and so this alliance was to be the first target of Western operations.

Operation Enduring Freedom consisted of a rapid air campaign in support of Afghanistan's local anti-Taliban ground forces. In addition, teams of special forces, primarily from the United States and the United Kingdom, were inserted alongside the Afghan Northern Alliance forces, with independent units carrying out reconnaissance deep in the interior. The Taliban resisted heavy air bombardments and the onslaught of the Northern Alliance for three weeks, and then, decimated, they collapsed. Soon they were being pursued southwards and eastwards, many making for the sanctuary of Pakistan's North-West Frontier province, where they could rely on fellow militants for support. Many Afghans chose to switch sides, and began to assist the Western special forces teams to track down the 'Arab-Afghans', as al-Qaeda were known locally.

On the eastern border of Afghanistan, the mountainous terrain made pursuit more difficult, and it was clear that al-Qaeda fighters and their allies were making use of extensive cave systems at Tora Bora to protect themselves from air attack. Special forces, guided by local tribesmen, began to flush out these nests and the remnants of al-Qaeda were driven across the Pakistan border. There, some were able to escape into the hills, but a number were rounded up and arrested by Pakistan's security forces. Meanwhile, Afghanistan began to establish a democratically elected government, a process of security sector reform and the disarmament of hostile factions that would, it was hoped, bring to an end decades of civil war.

Previous pages: **A British soldier tries to secure the site of a suicide attack in Afghanistan's southern Helmand Province, 19 October 2006.**

Unfortunately, insufficient resources were made available for the Afghans to complete the process rapidly, and by 2005 there was evidence that the Taliban were resurgent, with bomb attacks and shootings around the country.

The United Nations was keen to see a comprehensive process of nation-building initiated, and it insisted that the occupying powers assist in extending the writ of the Afghan government in Kabul over the whole country. In the south, particularly in Helmand province, narcotics had long been the mainstay of the local economy. In 2007, Afghanistan was the world's chief exporter of opium, with over 90 per cent of opiates (including heroin) originating in the country. Mafia-like bosses were using the drugs money to run gangs, pay off rivals, ensure patronage and murder their enemies. It was often unclear whether these bosses were genuine members of the Taliban, or simply used that title to gain credibility with the local population. In 2006, when the British Army was tasked with the support of a counter-narcotics programme and the extension of the Afghan government's jurisdiction into Helmand (the centre of poppy cultivation) it put them on a collision course with a number of vested interests. In fact, although the British did not realize it at the time, drug money was also being used by the lower echelons of the government to buy positions and patronage. Local police forces were getting payouts from drug barons, or were so badly paid by the government that they simply robbed local citizens. When the British arrived to back the authority of the police, a number of local people assumed they were there to make life even worse for them, and joined a nascent resistance.

At the moment the British were beginning their deployment to Helmand, the Taliban were readying their final offensive. They had been preparing for three years, and assumed that the Iraq War, which had tied down thousands of Western troops, would keep the coalition forces in a weakened state in Afghanistan. There had been months of booby-trap bombs, IEDs, assassinations and widespread intimidation. Local Afghans who refused to assist the Taliban were threatened, 'disciplined' and (should they refuse to cooperate) eventually shot. The Taliban were determined to ruin Western development projects and burnt down schools, threatened non-governmental organizations, and kidnapped family of wealthier families to exact a ransom. Targeting disgruntled communities, the Taliban offered to support them in return for loyalty to their cause. Now, the Taliban leaders felt that they could call on thousands of volunteers, including enthusiasts from Pakistani

Madrassahs (religious seminaries, some of which teach a radical version of Islam), to launch an offensive that would overwhelm the poorly trained Afghan security forces, and persuade the West to abandon Kabul.

Part of the Taliban offensive in May 2006 was focused on the Arghandab Valley, north of Kandahar. Here the insurgents had established a base of operations and planned to strike against the city where their movement had first emerged in 1994. The Canadian troops in Kandahar were aware of the Taliban build-up, and faced a tough fight to avoid civilian losses while taking on increasing numbers of fighters.

At the same time, the British had arrived in brigade strength in Helmand and established a base at Camp Bastion near the provincial capital of Lashkar Gah. Although the British 16 Air Assault Brigade planned to adopt a 'light footprint' approach and win over the local population with a low-key presence, they were asked by the Provincial Governor to establish small posts around the province that would signal that the government of Afghanistan was the only legitimate authority. In counter-insurgency doctrine, it is established that small areas need to be

At Wanat, an outnumbered American detachment fought tooth and nail to defend their beleaguered patrol base. In Helmand, British troops found their small platoon houses under attack during a major Taliban counter-offensive towards Kandahar. These handfuls of plucky troops held on to their flimsy defences and inflicted major defeats on the Taliban.

occupied and improvements made to security and economy before the 'ink spot' of secure and pacified space is extended to new areas. Establishing small posts around the province risked 'penny-packeting' the British force. If one or two posts came under attack, it would be far harder to protect or reinforce them. The brigade commander tried to dissuade the Afghan Governor, but, given that the mission was to let the host nation authorities lead, he had no choice but to comply.

The plan was therefore to establish areas of responsibility, and, given the lack of manpower available and the desire to maintain a low profile, each would be protected by relatively small groups of men in fortified posts known as platoon houses or patrol bases. These had the advantage of being close to areas of population, presenting the opportunity to meet with and perhaps win over the local community, as well as protect the local bazaar and its economic activity. There was also a better chance of being able to control the roads and tracks, in conjunction with the local police. It soon became apparent, however, that some of the local police were in league with the Taliban, and no sooner had the bases been established than they came under attack.

The British in northern Helmand were surprised by the ferocity of these initial assaults. Dozens of Afghans would rush forward, bringing fire to bear from multiple positions and advancing on several axes. Rocket-propelled grenades (RPGs) would slam into the hastily built bunkers, and bullets from Kalashnikov assault rifles rained in. On other occasions, some Taliban would try to ambush a foot patrol, or fire on a base and then disappear; this 'shoot and scoot' tactic exhausted the British troops. At other times, there were more sustained attempts to overrun the platoon houses. Gun battles lasted hours, sometimes days, without relenting. As soon as the shooting died down, the British soldiers were expected to fill sandbags, repair their battered fortifications or get out on patrol. More and more frequently the patrols got 'bumped', that is, ambushed and attacked. As soon as the British fell back, the Taliban would swarm after them. To defend the posts, every available weapon was brought to bear – the rifle, the General Purpose Machine Gun, Browning .50 calibre heavy machine guns, sniper rifles and even Javelin missiles, which would normally be employed against armoured vehicles. The longer-range weapons proved invaluable in the destruction of buildings that provided the Taliban with cover or concealed their assembly areas. The Taliban, however, seemed undeterred by the casualties they were taking.

Attacks would often build quickly. A few RPG rounds would scream in, and the British soldiers would shout warnings to each other. Those manning the heavy weapons or on sentry duty would already be in action, while others (ostensibly resting but constantly on duty in case of an attack), would rush to a waist-high parapet or a sandbag wall. Rounds would pour in from multiple firing points, and the familiar sounds of battle – the 'crack-ping' of a near miss, or the 'crack-thud' of rounds whacking into sandbags – would be heard by all. There would also be an occasional cheer, as British troops confirmed a kill or saw the spectacular results of a close air support mission that they had called in. The firefights lasted on into the night, with individual Taliban fighters trying to work their way in to shoot at a closer range. Sometimes fire was exchanged within yards of the patrol base walls.

After some weeks of continuous fighting, the British had to decide whether they were achieving their mission or simply incurring great risks for no strategic results. The danger that a helicopter might be lost seemed particularly acute when, at this early stage of the campaign, there were so few of them. There was an alarming rise in the number of 'mine-strikes' (number of mines detonated by vehicle patrols) and so helicopters were becoming the preferred mode of transport to get ammunition and food in, and the wounded out. The situation seemed even more desperate when a step change in the skills and abilities of the Taliban was noticed. The British suspected that the sudden improvement in the accuracy of mortar, RPG and sniper fire was the result of external support. Either the Taliban were getting assistance in the form of trained personnel, or perhaps they were receiving new weapons and equipment, such as sniper rifles and night vision gear – or perhaps both. Some evidence suggested that Pakistan was being used as a conduit for these specialist tools and operatives.

The result was a change of British tactics. Platoon houses were consolidated and reinforced. More troops were brought into the fight. When the Royal Marine Commandos were deployed, they took advantage of the traditional winter lull in activity to take the fight to the enemy, and, treating the open areas of *dasht* (desert) like the open sea, they established a more aggressive and fluid patrol pattern that gave them back their mobility. New doctrine was established too, and fresh efforts were made to win the support of local leaders and farmers, but violence in Helmand remained at a higher level than in any other province of the country. By 2009, American Marines had joined the British and they began to secure the north and west, allowing the British to concentrate their forces in the centre and more densely populated valleys. There was now the chance to carry out a traditional counter-insurgency strategy, namely to shape (influence the population), clear (drive out the insurgents), hold and build (making improvements to local infrastructure). When the Taliban kept up their violent disruption and intimidation, it was clear it was going to be a long fight.

Similar challenges faced American forces in Afghanistan. As dawn broke on 13 July 2008, the Taliban attacked an American Regional Command East outpost in Kunar province, close to the Pakistan border, and fought a short, sharp battle that left 9 Americans and more than 30 jihadist fighters dead. The US troops were drawn from 2nd Platoon, Chosen Company, 2nd Battalion, 503rd Infantry Regiment, which was part of the 173rd Airborne Brigade. This force of 45 men had begun building a patrol house in the Waygul Valley, close to the village of Wanat. Three US Marines had joined the outpost in order to continue the training of a dozen Afghan National Army soldiers. As the work progressed, successive days of bad weather prevented any air cover, which gave the Taliban the opportunity to approach the base unde-tected, concentrating from distant hideouts through small valleys and nearby gullies. As the Taliban reached their final assembly area at night, they opened an irrigation dam so the sound of rushing water would cover the noise of their foot-steps and whispers. Some Taliban fighters managed to locate the Claymore mines on the approaches to the base, and turned them around. Others used previous recon-naissance intelligence to point out the positions of American heavy weapons.

When the battle commenced, the American base was still far from complete. There had not been time to build entrenched observation posts on high ground around the compound. There was a lack of construction materials, and, because of the high Afghan summer temperatures and intense work required, the garrison had almost run out of water. The dangerous situation had arisen during an American attempt to win the hearts and minds of local Afghans. The US forces had previously been talking to village elders for several weeks, trying to persuade them to allow the base to be built in Wanat. It seems that the Taliban got wind of the discussions, and used this negotiation time to prepare a major attack that struck the base before it was fully operational. This setback was typical, and shows how difficult the Americans had found conducting a classic counter-insurgency campaign: all too often they were engaged in firefights and battling for their survival, rather than 'winning hearts and minds'. The shortage of troops and the nature of the fighting meant that base security had to be provided by the same troops engaged in construction. This meant round-the-clock labouring for tired men, and it also suggested that it would be difficult to mount enough patrols beyond the new base to dominate the ground and deter attacks. The Americans were eager to find and arm local tribesmen who would work with them in order to increase the allied forces available, but there simply weren't enough US troops to cover every valley and protect every community from Taliban fighters who would slip across the Afghan–Pakistan border with relative ease.

At 0420 hours, in the grey first light of dawn, volleys of RPGs began to strike the half-constructed base. This was the preliminary bombardment to an assault by between one and two hundred Taliban, significantly outnumbering the American garrison. The first salvos concentrated on the American's heavy weapons (namely a 120 mm mortar, a guided anti-tank missile system and a .50 calibre machine gun). One soldier described the barrage as feeling like 'a thousand RPGs at once'. With the heavy weapons knocked out, the Taliban rushed forward to fight at close quarters in order to make it impossible for the Americans to call in airstrikes. The attack had been planned in great detail. The Taliban threw rocks into the American trenches, hoping they would mistake them for grenades and jump out, whereupon they could be killed. Then the Taliban closed in from several directions, bringing as much fire to bear as possible. The Americans were simply unable to move because of the weight of fire smashing down onto their positions.

One soldier described the intensity of the battle: 'I continued to lay suppressive fire with the 240 [machine gun] but it was difficult because I was unable to stand due to wounds in both legs and my left arm.' When this soldier ran out of ammunition he realized he was the only one still alive in his corner of the patrol base. The Taliban were so close he could hear them talking.

Each American soldier was dependent on the battle skills practised back in the United States and honed by weeks of small-scale firefights in Afghanistan's hills. Men operated in pairs, each laying suppressive fire to cover the movement of the other. As the Taliban tried to move into the base, they were forced to leave their cover, or were silhouetted against the sky, presenting a clear target. It required considerable courage to take the aimed shots required to pick off the skirmishing fighters, but the Americans cut down the Taliban as they tried to swarm across the perimeter. Fortunately, the .50

calibre machine gun had survived the initial barrage, and its reassuring repetitive low thuds could be heard in action above the din of battle. Hundreds of rounds were expended. The Taliban knew it would take at least thirty minutes for American air support to become available, and this made them even more determined to overrun the position before there were retaliatory airstrikes. The fighters knew they were running out of time, but the battle continued for an hour before the jihadists had had enough and began to move away. The exhausted defenders were too preoccupied with identifying who was still alive and tending the wounded to pursue them.

Some 9 Americans were killed and another 27 were injured (representing 75 per cent of the initial strength of the post), but the Taliban also took heavy losses: it was estimated that between 21 and 52 insurgents were killed by the determined defenders. The final death toll could not be verified as the Taliban tried to extract many of their dead and wounded, leaving only trails of blood. Despite the desperate and close-quarter nature of the fighting, the Americans had held their new base. The Taliban had failed to complete their mission. They had no propaganda victory to crow about to their adherents, and they had lost a number of dedicated comrades. Often the Taliban complained about the strength of American firepower, and expressed a desire to fight on equal terms, but here, battling man for man, they had been held in check. Even with the element of surprise, greater numbers and all the intelligence they needed, and therefore the best odds of victory, they had been unable to overrun the Americans.

In both the British and American cases, relatively small numbers of well-armed and well-equipped Western forces had been able to hold off larger numbers of Taliban fighters, even though the fighters had the advantage in terms of the ground, initiative and sometimes in the abundance of weaponry. Although isolated and forced to rely on their own resources, the British and the Americans had defended themselves and denied their enemies any physical or ideological victory. The Afghan people may tire of the repeated jihadist promises of liberation, of their strict and brutal precepts, and of the threats that follow when the Taliban fail to deliver. Alternatively, they may side with the fighters on the basis that the West may one day simply abandon the Afghan government. The Taliban are, after all, their countrymen. That chapter has not yet been written, but already the individual courage and collective endurance of the Western forces against the odds has etched the Afghan campaign of the early twenty-first century into that country's history.

CONCLUSION

Which factors enabled relatively small forces to achieve such dramatic results against all odds? It is tempting to construct a theory that links together a number of features common to the examples given here, but such a theory would be artificial and misleading. History indicates that the contingent is more important than apparent continuities, principles and laws. That said, while acknowledging the uniqueness of each of the circumstances presented in this book, it is possible to identify a number of themes and common features.

The obvious point is, perhaps, that the physical courage of the participants was crucial and outweighed other factors. In war, the physical commitment and bravery of those engaged in the fighting is so often more important than the weapons they carry or the training they receive – although these elements might instil a sense of confidence at times. In all the preceding examples, the courageous character of the small formations involved was crucial to the outcome. From Lieutenant Decatur leading a raiding party aboard the USS *Philadelphia* in 1803 to Force Zwicka fighting to the last tank on the Golan Heights in 1973, or the nameless French infantrymen who stuck by their emperor Napoleon in 1814, to the handfuls of 'Other Ranks' who held at bay the swarms of Taliban fighters in Afghanistan in 2009, the quality of individual bravery was critical.

Another factor we might identify in many of these examples is the placing of honour before everything else, including the risk of death or injury. At Camerone in 1863 and at Bois des Buttes in 1918, small numbers of troops were isolated, cut off and denied any hope of relief. Instead of surrendering, they chose to fight on, regardless of casualties, staying true to their professional duty. In both cases, they sought to buy time for comrades elsewhere, but even when this was achieved they chose to die with honour, rather than besmirch the name of their regiment. Individuals could have chosen to lie low and survive, and no one would have known – except themselves. As one veteran of war put it: '*I* would have noticed.'

In some cases, the elite status of units can make such commitment more likely, but that status is often based on self-perception and is not something officially bestowed by others. The special forces teams in Iraq in 2003 had high expectations of themselves, regardless of what others thought of them. When confronted by overwhelming odds, they believed this was a challenge for which they were prepared. Their training ensured they had specialist skills that enabled them to defeat larger and better-equipped adversaries, but these self-appointed attributes of honour and duty were clearly there too.

Certain military skills, such as the ability to manoeuvre coherently, the capacity to bring in a significant weight of fire or the endurance to move across the battlefield or campaign theatre at great speed, appear in other examples. Napoleon's campaign of 1814 was arguably one in which he and his army exercised these skills at their best. Despite overwhelming numbers of enemy forces advancing into France from several directions, Napoleon struck again and again, inspiring and winning devotion from his exhausted men at a time when defeat was imminent. The Six Days' Campaign was the epitome of the skilful fighting retreat against the odds. The ability to conduct the elaborate manoeuvres of war when exhausted was demonstrated by the UN forces surrounded at Chosin Reservoir in 1950. There, the American and British Marines, whose supplies had failed and who were subjected to a series of relentless assaults, were forced to rely on basic infantry battle drills (and the close coordination of armour or air power when available) to help extract themselves.

Another common feature of success against the odds was discipline. The ability to maintain cohesion and self-control – the characteristics of military discipline – have often enabled forces to suffer heavy casualties but continue to function effectively and confront a much stronger or more numerous enemy. At Kohima in 1944, British and Indian soldiers stood their ground against the determined assaults of the Imperial Japanese Army. Both sides possessed the firm discipline needed for success, but it was the Allied forces who, contrary to expectations, grimly endured the casualties, gruelling conditions and terror of repeated attacks to eventually succeed. Regiments and subunits held together because of the invisible bond between the men and the system of discipline that emphasized the synchronization of the individual within the whole organization. Survivors of the battle remarked that, even when death seemed certain, they knew they could not let their comrades down. Discipline helped them overcome the instinct for self-preservation. A similar effect of discipline combined with efficient organization enabled Major General Roberts to force march his army from Kabul to Kandahar over inhospitable terrain without any logistical support, and virtually without loss. Roberts' force was able to ward off the threat of Afghan attacks en route because his men, despite the heat and fatigue, maintained cohesion and discipline. They were then able to fight a significant battle straight off the line of march and relieve a beleaguered garrison.

In every example in this book, the troops displayed determination and perseverance. At Valley Forge in the American War of Independence, the core of the Continental army, despite a catalogue of defeats, endured irregular supplies, freezing conditions and unfamiliar and tedious training. When they emerged the following spring, their example inspired others to rejoin the revolutionary cause such that, within a few years, the Americans could field a regular army and secure victory at Yorktown.

At Bataan and at Stalingrad, many of the troops who withstood the fighting were there without choice. Cut off, the soldiers were in no position to withdraw, but what is surely remarkable is that they chose not to surrender, but to fight on. Indeed, wherever possible they took the fight to the enemy. In both examples, the level of respect between the belligerents was very low, and surrender to their enemies was thought to be practically pointless. As a result, many soldiers chose to fight on rather than face execution or death through neglect and brutality in a prison camp.

In certain cases, inspiring and effective leadership was important to the success of a smaller or weaker force. At Antietam in 1862, the weight of fire that swept the open ground before Burnside's Bridge made any forward movement impossible. Union troops had been pinned down and many of their officers killed or wounded. The courageous leadership of the colour party of the 51st Pennsylvania Regiment, who acted on their own initiative, was the spur to an advance that carried the bridge and the heights beyond, and, crucially, began to turn the tide of the entire battle. In South America, Simón Bolívar exhibited a very different sort of courage: the kind that endures and absorbs years of setbacks, inadequate resources and overwhelming odds. His final campaign to liberate Venezuela, which involved leading a tiny military expedition across some of the most challenging terrain in the world, earned him legendary status.

Effective leadership also characterized the guerrilla resistance of De Wet in the South African War – although critics suggest he merely prolonged the war without doing much damage to the British forces who opposed him. In fact, De Wet's contribution was to inspire the Afrikaners to keep their cause alive with a patriotic zeal bordering on religious devotion. He was able to delay the British victory, increase the costs they had to bear, and constantly evade their attempts to snare him. His ability to escape earned the respect of (and even amused) his enemies.

The concept of a cause for which men were fighting was evident in a number of other examples. National liberation was the stated aim of the Greeks in the war for independence, though it is quite clear that many Greeks felt more strongly about the religious difference with the Turks, than about possessing a strong sense of national unity. Indeed, this was borne out in the episode of civil war that broke out while the war for independence was still in progress. Despite this, the cause was appealing to many intellectuals in Western Europe, and the popularization of the liberation struggle pushed governments towards armed intervention.

The sense of resistance with a last-ditch effort has also inspired small numbers of men and women to achieve success against all odds. Piłsudski's subordinate commanders on the eve of the Battle of Warsaw in 1920 were not convinced that the plan of their general would work, but they threw themselves into the execution of the operation because their defeat seemed imminent. The Finns in 1940 also knew that the odds against them were tremendous, but by combining a do or die attitude with skills that were appropriate to the climate and terrain (namely light infantry manoeuvres on skis and defence in depth) they fought the Soviet army to a virtual standstill. The surviving tank crews on the Golan in 1973 also utilized their skills and fought in the belief this was a last-ditch defence of their country. Despite suffering heavy casualties they were able to continue fighting.

Being in a defensive stance clearly increased the advantages for a number of the small groups described in this book, though a fixed position does not automatically mean that success is assured, of course. Defensive positions could be bypassed, neutralized with fire or simply encircled and deprived of supplies. But when their adversaries need to force a passage through a defensive zone, and the defenders possess the means and the will to contest the battlefield, then smaller or apparently weaker forces can make effective use of the terrain, climate or protection of natural and man-made features. The hacienda at Camerone, the trenches of Bois des Buttes, the Mannerheim Line in Finland, the Bataan Peninsula, the factories and streets of Stalingrad, the ridge at Kohima, the Toktong Pass near the Chosin Reservoir, the bunkers along the Golan Heights, and the patrol bases of Afghanistan all provided just enough protection to enable their defenders to hold on against superior forces just long enough to achieve their aims.

It was the certainty of victory, being on the offensive and the conviction that they would prevail, which inspired the British and Indian forces on the ridge at Delhi in 1857. It was the daring of Lieutenants Decatur and O'Bannon, seeking revenge against pirates and the loss of the *Philadelphia*, that gave the American navy and marines the edge in their raids of 1804–5. The Union troops at Burnside's Bridge wanted to get forward, and their momentum carried them on to their objectives, while General Roberts' soldiers never doubted the ability of their commander to drive on, avenge their comrades at Maiwand and achieve victory over the Afghans. That confidence in their status and offensive capability was still the theme for the special forces teams in Iraq in 2003.

These examples show that in both defence and attack, the characteristics of the forces involved can affect the outcome of any engagement. Weapon types, the right manoeuvres and appropriate logistics are all important, but they are inconsequential without the qualities of leadership, determination and physical courage. It is these that have formed the basis of this book, and each of them, perhaps, can inspire us in our own endeavours.

FURTHER READING

1 /// GEORGE WASHINGTON AND THE AMERICAN PATRIOTS AT YORKTOWN, 1781

Abbott, W. W., et al (eds), *The Papers of George Washington, 1748–1799*, 52 vols to date (Charlottesville, 1976–)

Alden, J. R., *George Washington: a Biography* (Baton Rouge, 1984)

Black, J. (ed.), *Great Military Leaders and their Campaigns* (London and New York, 2008)

—— *War for America: the Fight for Independence* (New York, 1991)

Carp, E. W., *To Starve the Army at Pleasure: Continental Army Administration and American Political Culture, 1775–1783* (Chapel Hill, 1984)

Ellis, J. J., *His Excellency: George Washington* (New York, 2004)

Ferling, J. E., *The First of Men: a Life of George Washington* (Knoxville, 1988)

Freeman, D. S., *George Washington: a Biography*, 7 vols (New York, 1948–57)

Higginbotham, D., *George Washington and the American Military Tradition* (Athens, 1985)

Royster, C., *A Revolutionary People at War: the Continental Army and the American Character, 1775–1783* (Chapel Hill, 1979)

2 /// THE UNITED STATES MARINES AT TRIPOLI, 1803–5

Fremont-Barnes, G., *The Wars of the Barbary Pirates* (New York and Oxford, 2006)

Kitzen, M. L. S., *Tripoli and the United States at War: a History of American Relations with the Barbary States, 1785–1805* (London, 1993)

Lambert, F., *The Barbary Wars: American Independence in the Atlantic World* (New York, 2005)

Simmons, E., *The United States Marines: a History*, 4th ed. (Annapolis, 2003)

3 /// NAPOLEON'S SIX DAYS' CAMPAIGN, FRANCE, 1814

Black, J. (ed.), *Great Military Leaders and their Campaigns* (London and New York, 2008)

Chandler, D., *On the Napoleonic Wars: Collected Essays* (London, 1994)

Esdaile, C., *The Peninsular War: a New History* (London, 2003)

Lachouque, H., *Napoleon en 1814* (Paris, 1959)

Leggiere, M., *The Fall of Napoleon: Volume 1, the Allied Invasion of France, 1813–1814* (Cambridge, 2007)

Miquel, P., *La Compagne de France de Napoleon, ou, Les Eclairs du Génie* (Paris, 1991)

Petre, F. L., *Napoleon at Bay* (New York, 1914)

Rothenberg, G. E., *The Art of Warfare in the Age of Napoleon* (Bloomington, 1980)

—— *The Napoleonic Wars* (New York, 2005)

Schneid, F. C., *Napoleon's Conquest of Europe: the War of the Third Coalition* (Westport, 2005)

4 /// SIMÓN BOLÍVAR AND THE LIBERATION MOVEMENT, SOUTH AMERICA, 1813–25

Black, J. (ed.), *Great Military Leaders and their Campaigns* (London and New York, 2008)

Bushnell, D., *Simón Bolívar: Liberation and Disappointment* (London and New York, 2004)

De Grummond, J. and R. Slatta, *Simón Bolívar's Quest for Glory* (Texas, 2003)

Lynch, J., *Simón Bolívar: A Life* (New Haven, 2006)

Mansur, G., *Simón Bolívar* (Albuquerque, 1969)

O'Leary, D. F., *Bolívar and the War of Independence: Memorias del General Daniel Florencio O'Leary*, trans. and ed. R. F. McNerney, Jr (Austin and London, 1970)

5 /// THE WAR FOR INDEPENDENCE, GREECE, 1821–29

Brewer, D., *The Greek War of Independence: the Struggle for Freedom from the Ottoman Oppression and the Birth of the Modern Greek Nation* (Woodstock, 2001)

Paroulakis, P. H., *The Greek War of Independence* (Darwin, 2000)

Woodhouse, C. M., *The Greek War of Independence: its Historical Setting* (New York, 1975)

6 /// THE BRITISH ARMY AT DELHI, INDIA, 1857

David, S., *The Indian Mutiny* (London, 2002)

Edwardes, M., *Battles of the Indian Mutiny* (London and New York, 1963)

Hibbert, C., *The Great Mutiny: India, 1857* (London and New York, 1978)

Rice Holmes, T., *A History of the Indian Mutiny* (London, 1904)

7 /// THE BATTLE OF BURNSIDE'S BRIDGE AT ANTIETAM, AMERICA, 1862

Bailey, R. H., *The Bloodiest Day: Antietam* (Alexandria, 1984)

Gallagher, G., *The American Civil War: War in the East* (Oxford, 2001)

McPherson, J. M., *Crossroads of Freedom: Antietam* (New York and Oxford, 2002)

Murfin, J. V., *The Gleam of Bayonets: the Battle of Antietam and the Maryland Campaign of 1862* (New York, 1965)

8 /// THE FRENCH FOREIGN LEGION AT THE BATTLE OF CAMERONE, MEXICO, 1863

Brunon, J., *Camerone* (Paris, 1988)

Patay, M., *Camerone* (Paris, 1981)

Rickards, C., *The Hand of Captain Danjou: Camerone and the French Foreign Legion in Mexico, 30 April 1863* (Ramsbury, 2005)

Ryan, J. C., *Camerone: The French Foreign Legion's Greatest Battle* (Westport, 1996)

9 /// LORD ROBERTS AND THE MARCH FROM KABUL TO KANDAHAR, AFGHANISTAN, 1879–80

Heathcote, T. A., *The Afghan Wars, 1838–1919* (Staplehurst, 2003)

Hopkins, B. D., *The Making of Modern Afghanistan* (Basingstoke and New York, 2008)

Robson, B., *The Road to Kabul: the Second Afghan War, 1878–1881* (London and New York, 1986)

Tanner, S., *Afghanistan: a Military History from Alexander the Great to the Fall of the Taliban* (Cambridge, 2003)

10 /// CHRISTIAAN DE WET AND BOER RESISTANCE, SOUTH AFRICA, 1900–2

Judd, D. and K. T. Surridge, *The Boer War* (New York, 2003)

Pakenham, T., *The Boer War* (London and New York, 1979)

Pretorius, F., *The A to Z of the Anglo–Boer War* (Lanham, 2010)

—— *The Great Escape of the Boer Pimpernel Christiaan de Wet: the Making of a Legend* (Johannesburg, 2001)

11 /// THE DEVONS AT BOIS DES BUTTES, FRANCE, 1918

Colvill, R. A., *Through Hell to Victory: from Passchendaele to Mons with the 2nd Devons in 1918* (Torquay, 1927)

Robinson, R. E. R., *The Bloody Eleventh: History of the Devonshire Regiment* (Exeter, 1988)

Taylor, J., *The Devons. A History of the Devonshire Regiment, 1685–1945* (Bristol, 1951)

12 /// THE BATTLE OF WARSAW, POLAND, 1920

Fuller, J. F. C., *The Battle of Warsaw, 1920* (London, 1970)

Piłsudski, J. and M. N. Tuchachevskii, *1920 and its Climax: The Battle of Warsaw During the Polish-Soviet War, 1919–1920* (London and New York, 1972)

Zamoyski, A., *Warsaw 1920: Lenin's Failed Conquest of Europe* (London, 2008)

13 /// THE WINTER WAR, FINLAND, 1939–40

Delf, B. and B. Irincheev, *The Mannerheim Line, 1920–39: Finnish fortifications of the Winter War* (Oxford and New York, 2009)

Screen, J. E. O., *Mannerheim: the Finnish Years* (London, 2000)

Trotter, W., *A Frozen Hell: the Russo–Finnish Winter War of 1938* (Chapel Hill, 1991)

14 /// THE BATTLE FOR THE BATAAN PENINSULA, PHILIPPINES, 1941–42

Connaughton, R., *MacArthur and Defeat in the Phillipines* (College Station, 2003)

Mallonnee, R. C., *Battle of Bataan: An Eyewitness Account* (New York, 2003)

Young, D. J., *The Battle of Bataan: A Complete History*, 2nd ed. (Jefferson, 2009)

15 /// THE STRUGGLE FOR STALINGRAD, RUSSIA, 1942–43

Antill, D., and P. Dennis, *Stalingrad 1942* (New York and Oxford, 2007)

Beevor, A., *Stalingrad* (London, 1999)

Black, J. (ed.), *The Seventy Great Battles of All Time* (London and New York, 2005)

Craig, W., *Enemy at the Gates: the Battle for Stalingrad* (New York, 1973)

Glantz, D. M., and J. M. House., *When Titans Clashed: How the Red Army Stopped Hitler* (Kansas, 1995)

Jones, M. K., *Stalingrad: How the Red Army Survived the German Onslaught* (Philadelphia, 2007)

16 /// THE DEFENCE OF KOHIMA, BURMA–INDIA BORDER, 1944

Lyman, R., *Kohima 1944: the Battle that Saved India* (Oxford, 2010)

Slim, W., *Defeat into Victory* (London, 1971)

17 /// THE RETREAT FROM CHOSIN RESERVOIR, KOREA, 1950

Owen, J., *Colder Than Hell: a Marine Rifle Company at Chosin Reservoir* (Annapolis, 2000)

Russ, M., *Breakout: Chosin Reservoir, Korea, 1950* (New York, 1998)

Sandler, S., *The Korean War: No Victors, No Vanquished* (London, 1999)

18 /// THE DEFENCE OF THE GOLAN HEIGHTS, ISRAEL, 1973

Herzog, C., *The Arab–Israeli Wars: War and Peace in the Middle East* (London, 2005 rev. edn)

—— *The War of Atonement: the Inside Story of the Yom Kippur War* (London, 1975)

Insight Team of the London Sunday Times, *The Yom Kippur War* (New York, 1974)

Johnson, R., J. France and M. Whitby, *How to Win on the Battlefield* (London and New York, 2010)

Van Creveld, M., *Military Lessons of the Yom Kippur War: Historical Perspectives* (Beverly Hills, 1975)

19 /// THE BATTLE OF DEBECKA, IRAQ, 2003

Antenori, F. and H. Halberstadt, *Roughneck Nine–One* (New York, 2006)

Black, J. (ed.), *The Seventy Great Battles of All Time* (London and New York, 2005)

Neville, L., *Special Operations Forces in Iraq* (New York and Oxford, 2008)

20 /// THE DEFENCE OF THE PLATOON HOUSES AND THE BATTLE OF WANAT, AFGHANISTAN, 2006–8

Bishop, P., *3 Para* (London, 2007)

Grey, S., *Operation Snakebite* (London, 2009)

SOURCES OF ILLUSTRATIONS

INDEX

//